Advance Praise for

CELESTIAL WISDO

FOR EVERY YEAR OF YOUR LIFE

"Z Budapest and Diana L. Paxson successfully combine their extensive experience and 'knowing' to create the first comprehensive and easy-to-follow cosmic road map for the soul. What's more, they've flagged all the rough roads, hair-raising turns and deep potholes scattered along your soul's bumpy journey. And there is sheer delight in the learning. This is compelling, absorbing and absolutely impossible to put down!"

> —C.C. BRONDWIN, author of *Clan of the Goddess: Celtic Wisdom and Ritual for Women* and *Maiden Magick: A Teen's Guide to Goddess Wisdom Ritual*

"This excellent book is the ultimate astrological birthday guide. It reveals clever ways to celebrate all the special birthdays in your life. This book knows what's coming up and how to celebrate it!"

> —SOPHIA, author of *The Little Book of Hot Love Spells* and *The Girlfriend's Guide to Goddess Empowerment*

"Each ritual savors the gems sifted from the year-birthdays become touchstones that enliven our lives."

> —NANCY BRADY CUNNINGHAM, co-author of *Tarot Celebrations* and *A Book of Women's Altars*

CELESTIAL WISDOM

FOR EVERY YEAR OF YOUR LIFE

Also by Z Budapest

The Holy Book of Women's Mysteries
The Grandmother of Time
Grandmother Moon
The Goddess in the Office
The Goddess in the Bedroom
Summoning the Fates

Also by Diana L. Paxson

Priestess of Avalon (with Marion Zimmer Bradley)
The Serpent's Tooth

Hallowed Isle Series
The Book of the Sword
The Book of the Spear
The Book of the Caldron
The Book of the Stone

Z BUDAPEST & DIANA L. PAXSON

CELESTIAL WISDOM

FOR **EVERY YEAR** OF **YOUR LIFE**

Discover the Hidden Meaning of Your Age

WEISER BOOKS
Boston, MA/York Beach, ME

First published in 2003 by
Red Wheel/Weiser, LLC
York Beach, ME
With offices at:
368 Congress Street
Boston, MA 02210
www.redwheelweiser.com

Cataloging-in-Publication Data available upon request from the Library of Congress.

ISBN 1-57863-282-X

Typeset in EideticNeo, Caslon Antique and Interstate

Printed in Canada

TCP

10 09 08 07 06 05 04 03
8 7 6 5 4 3 2 1

We dedicate this work to the divine Three
who spin on the Wheel of Life.
To Energy, Matter, and Meaning—
the sisters intertwined.
May they bless humanity with bright
and hopeful insights. Blessed be.

CONTENTS

Acknowledgments xi

Introduction 1

Birth and Before: Beginning the Journey 11

Ages 1 to 10: First Flowering 21

Ages 11 to 20: It Was the Best of Times,
It Was the Worst of Times 43

Ages 21 to 30: Brave New World 65

Ages 31 to 40: Carousel 91

Ages 41 to 50: Crisis and Crown 113

Ages 51 to 60: The Age of Sovereignty 139

Ages 61 to 70: Older or Elder? 163

Ages 71 to 80: The Secret Country 187

Ages 81 to 90 and Beyond: The Age
of Enlightenment 207

Afterword 227

Glossary 233

Resources 237

ACKNOWLEDGMENTS

W E WOULD LIKE TO EXPRESS OUR debt and our gratitude to Margaret Cole, Adric Petrucelli, and Wendy Ashley for their astrological advice. We must also thank the many women and men of all ages who were willing to share their experiences, their insights, and their dreams with us. Their contributions helped us to put our own memories into perspective and provided a foundation for this book that was both broader and richer than anything we could have created alone.

INTRODUCTION

THIS IS A BOOK FOR EVERY WOMAN who has ever had a birthday. It used to be that the most dreaded question a woman could be asked was, "How old are you?" When Diana's mother had a birthday, she would say that she was "seven hundred years old" to evade the question. Women would lie desperately, hoping nobody would remember how long ago that great party they had to celebrate their thirtieth birthday really was.

As the old joke goes, if you don't like getting older, consider the alternative! Celebrating each of your birthdays as the triumph it is can help you to live a life in which each year has meaning.

With our first birthday, we leave the special world of babyhood and join the human family. The increasing life span of the human race will give many of us close to a hundred chances for more. What will we do with these years? What challenges will we face, and how can we deal with them? What is our destiny?

Everything that exists is part of a system in which it has a place and function. Whether or not one believes in a divine source for this system—Goddess or God or Higher Power—it is clear that the system itself is purposeful and practical and coordinates the entire universe. Some things influence all of us—historical events, cultural evolution, and the movements of those planets that affect everyone born within a generation. Other planetary cycles give structure to individual lives— in particular, the Saturn Cycle, which divides each life into three, or, if you live long enough, four destinies, each with a different mission to fulfill. Saturn is the hinge of fate—its energy swings us through the door between destinies. Each destiny brings us a new mission.

Don't worry if the stars seem to be influencing your life on a some- what different schedule than the one we describe in this book. In Nature, things take their time. Every individual develops at her own natural speed. This book is not a set of tables that can announce exactly when the next tide will come in, but it will tell you when the next wave is near. The laws of Nature apply to everyone. Sooner or later the tide will reach you, and you'll go with the flow. Most of the time, it will even seem like your own idea!

Each one of us is given different chances and choices. Our families, friends, personal horoscopes, and, above all, the decisions we make during our lifetimes all interact with these more general influences to shape our lives.

Understanding Astrology

LIKE MANY OTHER DISCIPLINES, astrology has a number of traditions. We have chosen to work with tropical rather than sidereal astrology because it is the most popular.

OUR BIRTH CHARTS

No two people develop on exactly the same schedule, but when we organize the experience of individuals within an astrological framework, a pattern begins to emerge.

These days, most people have a basic acquaintance with astrological lingo. You probably know your *sun sign*—the constellation of the zodiac through which the sun was passing when you were born. The sun sign has a great deal to do with how we relate to the outside world. It may also define our deepest aspirations.

But the moon is highly important as well. Its position in the zodiac determines how our personalities will be perceived, how we deal with emotions, and how we relate to others. It may predict the kinds of emotional cycles that will affect us, as well as certain aspects of health and living situations. In addition to the *moon sign,* the *nodes* of the moon, the points where the moon's orbit intersects the path of the sun, move backward through the zodiac, affecting both the possibility of growth and inhibiting habit patterns.

The third influence is the sign of the zodiac that is rising at the moment of birth, which determines how we present ourselves to the world. It is the window through which we look out at the world, and through which the world looks at us. The *rising sign* changes swiftly, so that twins born a few minutes apart can have very different personalities. Since the rising sign is a strong influence on styles of behavior, it may affect the role we play in our families or in organizations.

These are the Big Three of our charts, followed by the planets, whose position in relation to the zodiac and to each other create the network of influences that modify the effects of the sun, moon, and rising sign. Getting your chart done by a competent astrologer can illuminate many aspects of your life. Or you can use one of the many astrological programs on the Internet to print out your own. Two good sites to check out are www.alabe.com and www.astrology.net. Once you have your chart, there are many self-help books available to help you with the interpretation. Several are listed in the Resources at the end of this book.

PLUTO'S INFLUENCE

In addition to our personal horoscopes, we begin our lives under the influence of the planet Pluto, whose placement affects our entire generation. For instance, the "Baby Boom" generation was born while Pluto was in Leo (1938–1956), a sign that focuses on power and its use. The dark side of power, in the rise of dictators, and the redeeming movement to restore power to the people both come from the same source. From 1956 to 1972, Pluto was in Virgo, whose feminine influence supported a major increase in awareness of the need for improvement in areas such as women's rights and health care. The years 1972–1984 were the Libra generation, concerned with balance and equality. From 1985–1995 Pluto was in Scorpio—an awareness of sex and death dominated the news, particularly with the appearance of AIDS. Currently Pluto is moving through the sign of Sagittarius (1995–2008), the hybrid human/animal who is also the Wounded Healer. This is a time for advances in medicine and increase in humanitarian awareness.

Old hatreds will break out with a last, desperate violence, to be met with healing.

THE CYCLES OF THE PLANETS

As we move through life, the heavenly bodies follow their own courses, moving away from their positions on our birth charts and back again in an eternal dance. These cycles are called *transits*. Some of them affect us personally, while others can have an impact on entire generations. The transits of the slower planets—Pluto, Neptune, Uranus, and Saturn—have the greatest impact in activating the potential of our birth charts.

Pluto rules the generations, stirs up the depths and releases the deep-flowing, deadly passions. Pluto governs sex, rebirth, and death. Neptune is the Redeemer who stimulates our imaginations and activates a longing for spiritual awareness. Uranus rules the sign of Aquarius and the drive to evolve our species. The influence of this planet pushes us to speak and work on behalf of others, to serve, and to lead, to wake up human hearts, and allows change to seep through and reach everyone. Uranus guides us through the three Saturn destinies. And it is Saturn who is the Great Teacher who makes us mature, who teaches us how to live on earth and dream of heaven. Its symbol is half-fish and half-goat, with horns that touch the stars. Ready or not, Saturn brings us to the table where the other influences can give us the nourishment we need to change.

Saturn and the other planets may oppose their initial positions on the birth chart, causing difficulties in dealing with that energy. They may square them, which creates friction; form a sextile, which supports their energy; or make a trine, bringing new opportunity. The meaning of each period in our lives is shaped partly by these planetary movements, which bring in new influences and opportunities, and partly by the ways in which we choose to respond to them.

The length of the cycles for different planets varies. The planet Mars zips through the zodiac, returning to his natal position on your birth chart in a conjunction to re-energize us every two years. Jupiter, the Luck-Bringer, has a twelve-year cycle, renewing optimism and expanding our horizons. The nodes of the moon circle back through the zodiac every eighteen to nineteen years, revitalizing our emotions. Saturn, whose transit brings him back to his natal position approximately every twenty-eight years, is the "Celestial Taskmaster." When he turns the wheel it is time for us to take responsibility for our future and build a new destiny. For some this may constitute a virtual rebirth. Others may re-evaluate their goals and move into a new level of involvement, though they still have the same responsibilities. Uranus will only return once in our lifetimes, at age eighty-four, which completes one cycle of the personality. The cycle of Neptune, the Dream-Bringer, is too long for him to return at all, though he does have one opposition.

At the same time, their effect will be modified by an individual chart's configurations. So don't get confused if the events in your life don't seem to be following the plan laid out in this book. If everything else in our charts is working for success at a given time, neither squares nor oppositions will hamper us.

AGES, ERAS, AND SUB-AGES

An *age* can be the number of candles on our last birthday cake, or a period in our lives, or the era in which we live. Everyone who is alive today shares in the work of our Age, but our era is only one phase of larger movements—a Planet Age, a Galactic Age—of which we are an organic part. Without people, consciousness cannot evolve and civilizations cannot be born. All of us have a meaningful part to play. For some, the mission of our First or Second Destiny will be to reproduce the species. But all of us share the mission of improving life on Earth.

It is only when we are able to look at an entire lifetime that we can really appreciate the big picture. Not only are we better able to understand our own lives, but we can see them in the context of the era in which we have lived.

These eras are shaped by the great transpersonal planets, Pluto,

Neptune, Uranus, and Saturn, whose influence transcends individual destinies. These are the Big Four.

Finally, our lives are shaped by the great Astrological Ages that determine the rise and fall of civilizations. Within these greater cycles are sub-ages. We are moving toward the end of the Piscean Age, but it is the sub-age of Aquarius through which we are now passing at the beginning of the twenty-first century. The sub-age of Aquarius began in 1962 and will last for 175 years. An Aquarian influence strengthens the emergence of a humanistic consciousness. Today, the media is making the whole world an electronic village. We all witness events at the same time and share each other's reactions. Learning is accelerated. Although the true Age of Aquarius will not begin until the twenty-fourth century, our own sub-age is opening a window on that future dawning of global consciousness.

Finding Our Mission

A S HUMANS, WE HAVE A TRIPLE MISSION—a task that is given to us when Saturn's cycle presents us with each new destiny. There are many things in our lives that we have no power to change. We live in a given time and environment and are subject to the pressures of physiology, history, and the influences of the planets as they move through our charts. Together, these things shape our destinies. As teenagers, for instance, it is our *destiny* to pass through puberty. Part of our adolescent *mission* is to learn how to handle our sexuality. One might say that our destiny for a particular period in our lives consists of the "hand of cards" we are given. Our mission is to find the best possible way to play them.

Our first mission is to fulfill the larger destiny of our generation. We take on this mission by choosing the generation in which we will be born. The second is to contribute to the progress of the species. Many of us will do this by having children—the urge to do so is programmed into our biological clocks. But whether or not we bear children, for many our real contribution is through the work we do. Humans are no longer an endangered species focused primarily on the physical world. Now we need artists, philosophers, and leaders to teach us to be more evolved humans. The third mission is self-realization, to realize our full potential. It can take until we reach our mid-eighties, when Saturn returns to his natal position in our charts for the third time, to understand who we really are. These days, more and more people will live long enough to have an opportunity to do so.

Using This Book

THIS BOOK HAS SOMETHING TO SAY about every year of your life, from birth and before to ninety and beyond, organized into a chapter for each decade. At the beginning of each chapter you'll find a box listing "Fate Dates" for that decade—a summary of the major astrological influences and the ages at which they come into play. These influences are discussed in more detail throughout the chapter, in the sections that describe each year of the decade—along with advice, commentary, and stories from the many people we asked to tell us about their experiences at that age. Each year description is followed by a suggestion for a birthday celebration for that age. At the end of each chapter, we suggest a ritual to mark a major life passage that occurs during that decade.

THE FATE DATES

The Fate Dates provide brief overviews of the planetary influences that occur during each decade: the ages at which changes occur, the planet or celestial body influencing the change, and kinds of the changes one can expect. Readers can use the tables for quick reference, and then read about the planetary influences in greater depth in the individual age sections.

THE AGES

In this book, you'll find many references to astrological influences. Ecology studies the interrelationships of physical systems. Astrology looks at the spiritual relationships of the stars. The movements of the larger planets are reflected in revolutions and social changes; those of the smaller ones set us up for life changes. Sometimes the influence of the transpersonal planets that influence the destiny of a generation takes precedence. At other times, our lives are shaped by the movement of the planets in our personal horoscopes. Interweaving among all these movements, we make our choices and exercise our free will. And constantly moving among the other influences is the great imperative—to create and to love. Each age description focuses on the tendencies of that age given the interaction of all of these forces.

Astrology shows us the larger patterns that govern our lives; personal experiences illuminate their meaning. Then, with spells and rituals, we take charge of our own progress.

Once you have checked out your current age, browse forward and back. Relive your childhood; anticipate what is to come.

THE BIRTHDAYS

Children, of course, are very conscious of their birthdays. For a child, surviving each year is an achievement. The older we grow, the more quickly the years go by, but many Americans have continued the custom of having birthday parties into adulthood. The birthdays that open each decade are particularly significant. Everyone needs to be appreciated at least once a year, so birthdays can, and should, be celebrated at any age.

When you were a child, it was usually your mother who arranged your birthday parties. But what if *you* are the mother? What if you are living alone? No one should have to cook on her birthday! One way to deal with this is to create a "birthday club" with several women, or a few families, who celebrate together. If you have children, join forces with some other mothers. Assist them to put on parties for their children and take turns making the birthday dinner for each other. If you belong to a women's spirituality group or a club, add the celebration of birthdays to your schedule. If you live alone, find some other women with whom to create a "birthday circle."

THE LIFE STORIES

In each chapter you will find insights and wisdom from people who are the age you have just passed or are about to be, who like you are seeking the spiritual dimension, the magical meaning of the stages through which we all must pass. As you read about their experiences, remember: In this test of life there are no wrong answers, though it helps if you ask the right questions! To tackle such a subject—an entire human life—needs more than one perspective. This book represents the combined efforts of two authors and the many women and some men who responded to our questionnaire. There were only two questions: "How does it feel to be this age?" and "What have you learned about life that you would like to share?"

As you read through the stories, you will be tempted to compare your experiences at different ages with those described. While some comments will sound like echoes of your own thoughts, others may not ring a bell at all. Don't worry—we all have the same destination, but there are many ways to reach it. No two people have exactly the same life story. But though you may not have had a certain experience at exactly the same time as our respondents, at many places in this book you will probably find statements that echo things that have happened to you. Whether you find in these stories a caution or an inspiration, remember, we are all companions on the road.

THE RITUALS

In addition to birthdays, there are other points—physical, social, or astrological—at which a ritual can focus the experience and ease the transition. Such a ritual helps one to accept, at the deepest level, the reality of and need for change. When you read the chapter for your decade, skip ahead and look at the ritual for that decade. You will want to wait to celebrate some of the rituals until the end of your decade, but most are designed to take place at the point during the decade where you feel you are making that particular passage.

In traditional cultures, most rites of passage are performed in a group setting because such transitions change one's relationship to the community and sometimes one's legal status as well. Family and friends, therefore, are invited to witness and celebrate the change. Such a ritual is also, of course, a great excuse for a good party! But the main purpose of a ritual is to transform the person going through it, so if you do not have a group to work with, consider working through the important parts of the ritual alone.

Remember, each year offers you a new opportunity to live your life so that it will have its fullest possible meaning.

BIRTH AND BEFORE
Beginning the Journey

LIFE BEGINS LONG BEFORE CONCEPTION. Our first decision is when to enter the fray of human existence. The historical period into which we are born will determine the emotional, political, and spiritual environment in which we live our lives. It's an important decision. Once we have chosen our parents and connected with a developing egg, we cannot change our minds. We have chosen the generation with which we will travel through life.

At the moment when we take our first breaths, Mother Nature equips us with everything we need to make our existence meaningful. In small kernels of DNA she has planted the instructions not only for the first few months of life, but for the unfolding of an entire lifetime. This small baby in the crib, holds the potential for a life of nearly a century. Nature has given us the destiny of carrying on the life of our species and of making our personal contribution to the unfolding history of our times.

Humans need a mission beyond simple survival. This mission is the mystery of our existence. A good mission fills us with pride, but sometimes only in hindsight can we see where an individual, or a generation, went wrong. Even then, memory and the historical record can preserve those negative examples, such as the atrocities of the past century, as a warning.

We all want to know what to expect from our lives. From Arnold Gesell's and Frances L. Ilg's *The Child from Five to Ten* to Gail Sheehy's *Passages,* books that chronicle the developments of each year and decade have helped us to understand what's going on now and what will happen next. Now it's time to look at our spiritual growth.

Mother Nature does not shove us out into the world without a map. She delegates guardians to watch our steps. She buries memories of her cycles deep in our souls. She has established checkpoints in our lives at which she can nudge us in the right direction. Our lives are a school, and each year teaches a new lesson.

Life is a mystery, but so is a layered cake or a cauldron of stew or the spiral structures of our DNA. But life is sacred, you may say—well, so, in our opinion, is a birthday cake or a stew. All things that creatively combine old elements to organize something useful and new are miracles.

Each cake and each stew is different, and so is each person, but there is a blueprint for life that applies to us all. A pattern begins to emerge. We do not exist independently of other entities in the universe. If this new century has taught us anything so far, it is that everything exists in relationship to everything else. Everything changes, voluntarily, or in response to the pressure of destiny.

In Classical Art, the Three Graces are often shown holding hands, dancing. Their dance is part of the circling of the heavens. Society changes, but the circle of life continues. Are these psychosocial alterations simply a function of social evolution, or could the movement of Pluto from Cancer to Leo have played a role? The circling of Saturn defines our major changes, but each year brings a new pattern, each age has its own significance.

Stepping into the Circle

HAVE YOU EVER THROWN UP YOUR HANDS in despair and shouted at the heavens, "What do you want with me? What am I doing here? Is there a plan?"

We've all felt that way at one time or another. The old joke that this life is only a test—if it were real, we would be given better directions—brings a rueful smile. There are times when everyone feels adrift or out of control. The cycles that govern cultures and nations are larger than those that affect a human lifetime, but they are just as powerful.

In order to understand where a book is going, we look at the table of contents. In the same way, the factors—genetic, environmental, and astrological—that are in place at the moment of birth provide the rough outline for our life stories. But as any author will tell you, an outline can tell you where a book is going, but only in the writing does one discover "how" it gets there. It is the meaning of a life that makes the difference.

Still, when you are trying to understand where you are going and how you got this far, starting with the factors that shaped you is a good plan.

The moment that officially begins our lives is the instant when we take that first breath. The array of influences—health and heredity, family environment, and the positions of the planets at that exact moment—set the pattern for our lives.

HEREDITY

Do our parents determine our destiny? Heredity certainly plays a role in what we become, but do genetics determine destiny?

Lucile's father was a Ph.D. in mathematics, but he had to tutor her all the way through high school math. Her mother had great artistic ability, and Lucile does too, but she didn't become an artist. Instead, she uses an ability to analyze events that is like her father's in her work as a scholar. Are her abilities inherited, or a reaction to her upbringing?

Carol's mother died of diabetes, and now she has it too. In this case, heredity has certainly played a role. But Carol is getting her condition under control through diet and exercise. If she's careful, she can live a long and active life.

As science unlocks the secrets of the human genome we will know more and more about the blueprint that creates our bodies. Coloring, height and weight and body type, health, and even intelligence may be inherited, giving us the resources with which we begin our lives, but the outcome depends on our choices, which are made by the spirit within.

As we grow older we can remember how it felt to be a child, although we now experience life very differently. It becomes clear that we are more than our bodies.

ENVIRONMENT

The environment into which we are born can be as important as our genes, starting with the world of the womb. The old controversy about the relative importance of nature and nurture takes on a new significance when we look at the influence of the spiritual as well as the physical environment, and consider the relationship among class, culture, and choice.

Certainly, someone who is sufficiently motivated can transcend an unprivileged early environment. Diana's father was born in Brooklyn to a working-class family with an alcoholic father. He had to go home from school across the roofs of the tenements to avoid the gangs, but his natural brilliance got him a good education. Even though the money he had earned working part-time jobs went to save his father's failing business, he arrived at Cal Tech with a scholarship and $5 and went on to earn a Ph.D.

But for every such success story there are many more who never succeed in breaking free. In the case of Diana's father, success was due not only to a high IQ, but to the care of his mother, who played chess with him and encouraged him to read. Where one factor is lacking, others may make up for it, but when a child is born with no advantages at all, success is difficult indeed. The prisons and streets are full of those who missed their chances or never had a chance at all. In such cases, those born with more blessings may find it good karma to offer what help is in their power.

Whatever fate gives us, life consists of a series of choices, and in the long run, success or failure depends on what we do with what we have. The more we know, the better our choices are likely to be.

Sometimes, meditation can give us information available no other way. Sande sent us this report on her experience during a trance journey to visit the Fates at one of Z's workshops:

> *I was adopted at birth by a childless couple in their mid-forties. He was Portuguese and she is Italian. My birth mother listed Scottish, English, and Irish as my maternal heritage. Because the adoption was private and through friends, I was able to ascertain that my biological father was Italian. I have seen pictures of my biological mother, grandmother, and great-grandmother (all deceased) and my biological siblings. My adoptive father's family was originally from the Azores, and family legend has it that my paternal great-grandmother was the village witch, as well as being a devout Catholic. My father said she scared him when he first met her.*
>
> *The first question I asked the Fates was if my past held anything important for me today. The answer was that my maternal great-grandmother was an important link for me, and then came the information that she and my adoptive father's grandmother the witch from Portugal were biologically related. I have always felt a strong bond with my adoptive father's family and look very much like some of my aunts, so this was not at all hard for me to accept.*
>
> *The second question related to my current life work and my "purpose." The answer . . . showed me as a light-generating being, a teacher of some sort, walking with women and children on open ground with a meadow and forest in view.*
>
> *The third question was directed toward my "becoming" and I*

*saw myself encased in heavy, metal armor. I was twirling toward
a meadow and as I twirled, the armor dropped off, one piece at a
time, until I was light and "free" and incredibly joyous.*

*I was able to discover more about the who and why of me
during the course of that meditation than in all the work I've
done so far.*

ASTROLOGY

The crucial moment, from the astrological point of view, is the minute
the baby takes its first breath. At that point responsibility for survival
passes from the mother to the child. We open ourselves to the energies of the world around us and begin the process that must continue
until we make our transition back to the Otherworld. Whatever else
happens in our lives, we have to keep breathing. The breath, therefore,
is our passport into this life, the existence we share with other living
things. Breath is sacred.

When the child takes her first breath, she draws in not only oxygen
but also the energy of the universe. The position of the planets at the
moment of birth will determine the psychic forces that accompany
her through life. This is why it is so important to take note of the time.
Even ten minutes' difference in the birth time of twins can affect the
way they relate to the world.

Astrology can be an important key to interpreting the script for
our lives, but we have to understand how to use it. It can be frustrating when the professional astrologer will say only that the stars offer
suggestions and opportunities, not certainties. It takes insight and
intuition to put all the pieces together and understand how they interact to offer us those choices. The stars do not "cause" us to have certain characteristics. Rather, their patterns are created by the same
forces that work upon our lives. The fluttering of the leaves does not
blow off your hat—it is the invisible wind that does both, and if you see
the grass flattening before you, you can guess that in another moment
the gust will hit you as well.

We exist in a universal vibrational soup. Most of it is invisible—we see only those things that reflect light. But there's a lot out there—we don't really know what reality truly contains, but we are slowly awakening to the importance of understanding everything, even those aspects that seem to make no sense at all. Do we really want to live in a world of complex chaos? There must be some organizing principle that will allow us to make sense of our times. We are surrounded by questions. What makes an Aquarian so accepting? What makes a Scorpio so stubborn? Why are some periods ripe for revolution while others, with equal injustices, stay calm? Are there really winds of war?

Destiny talks to us through the spirit of the times every day. We do not always listen, but it affects us whether we are consciously hearing it or not.

Beginning the First Destiny

THE MOMENT OF BIRTH is the official beginning of the First Destiny. Birth is the door between life and death. Until you emerge from your mother's womb you are not part of the world. To make the transition, you have to have a mother who invites you in. The newborn is a wrinkly helpless thing that can barely suck, plucked from a watery world where she has replayed within nine short months the entire evolutionary development of humankind.

To look upon a newborn is a thrilling experience. New babies have a strong spiritual aura, and if the Fates are kind, they will be placed in the arms of kind and loving mothers. The newborn child is a symbol of hope and the miracle of renewal. They are pure, without judgment or experience, beautiful, and vibrant. They remind us of our own beginnings.

Diana, who has assisted at a number of births, recalls the wonder of seeing the child emerge:

> *Except when I am actually watching it happen I find it hard to believe that every human being now in the world got here this way. The mound of the mother's belly knots and releases,*

*changing shape as the baby is pushed out. A woman is like the
Goddess when she gives birth, repeating the moment of creation.
Then the child is out, and you cut the cord that was its physical
connection to the mother. Now you've got a brand-new, separate
being, still trying to figure out what happened. But each baby
has its own way of reacting. When I first looked at my twin
grandchildren, one of them sleeping peacefully while the other
pushed and squirmed against the walls of the bassinet, it was
already clear which of them would find it easiest to get along in
the world.*

In the infant body is the potential to grow into a mature human being.
Everything you will need is tightly packed into your DNA files, ready to
kick in when the right time comes. You start with the basic script for
your life, but it's an outline only. How it plays out depends on you.

Birth Rites

P ROSPECTIVE PARENTS HAVE LITTLE CHOICE in the genetic heritage
they pass on, nor can they choose the moment of birth, but there
are ways to make the birth a rewarding spiritual experience that will
give parents and baby a good start to their life together.

If the birth is at home, set up an altar to the motherly power of the
Divine in the room where the birth will take place. Images of the
Madonna and Child, of Gaia, of Kuan Yin, or mother goddesses from
other cultures will inspire the right thoughts. Make the setting beautiful and keep lights at a restful level.

If the birth is taking place in a hospital or alternate birth center, a
simple altar (minus the fire) can be put up, and music can be played.
One or more of those assisting can intone "Ma" along with the mother's
grunts or moans. Chanting helps to focus everyone on the contraction
and can help transform a moan of pain into a positive sound. During
early stages, a gentle humming is relaxing. If the mother is used to
chanting, she may *Maaah* as well, especially during the pushing stage.

The sound will peak in intensity with the contraction, and it helps the mother to focus and direct her energy toward pushing out the child. Singing chants with appropriate words works well in some settings, especially if they are familiar to the mother.

If mother and doctor/midwife agree, the child's first bath may be in herb-scented water. Afterward, bless the child in a way appropriate to the family's religious tradition. A Christian would place the child under the protection of Jesus, or the Virgin Mary, and the angels. A Buddhist might call on Kuan Yin, and a pagan would call on the Great Mother and the four elements. The atmosphere immediately after the birth should be kept calm and peaceful, and the child should be kept in a dim, quiet place for the first few days, in contact with the mother's body as much as possible.

The Greek goddess Artemis, who drove the chariot of the moon, was also a goddess who assisted in birth and watched over the health and physical development of the growing child. At the time of the first full moon after the birth, if weather and health permit, take the infant outside and present her to the moon. You can make a prayer, such as:

> *Lady Moon with silver light,*
> *Radiant ruler of the night,*
> *Bless the child you've given me,*
> *As you bless the earth and sea.*

The Ritual

NAMING THE CHILD

Some say that each soul has many incarnations, and this birth is but a repetition of what has happened before. But even if this life is the only one, the human being, once born, does not remain the same. The infant becomes a child, the child the maiden, the maiden the woman, and the woman, the wisewoman.

Each stage is marked by physical and spiritual transformations. After birth, death is the greatest rite of passage of all. With each transformation the body changes. The experiences of the past seem to have happened to someone else. But the future is unknown. Everywhere, humans strive to ease these transitions by rites of passage. Most cultures have had some formal ritual to welcome a child as a member of the family and community. The following ritual welcomes a baby into a community of many beliefs and practices.

In addition to the parents and baby, participants should include sponsors (godparents) for the baby, and family and friends, including their children.

Bless the space by smudging or sprinkling with water or in the way appropriate to your tradition. Explain that you have invited everyone to witness your baby's naming, recognizing that this is only one of a series of rebirths and rites of passage that this soul will undergo.

Then the parents bring the child into the circle. First the mother and then the father give a brief description of health, physical characteristics, family background, artistic and cultural resources, and such that will be part of the child's inheritance from each side of the family. If a horoscope has been cast for the child, the astrologer presents it and summarizes its implications.

Next, the parents call upon those they have chosen as sponsors to help them carry the responsibility of raising the child. Each one is asked if he or she will pledge to love and care for the child on behalf of the community, and indicates acceptance by taking the baby into his or her arms.

All the children present come up and, if there are enough of them, make a circle around the parents and the baby. They may sing the following chant to the tune of "Twinkle, twinkle, little star...":

> Brother (or Sister), welcome here today—
> Grow up soon so we can play!

When the children and the sponsors have resumed their places in the circle, it is time to give the child a name. Give each child a piece of candy to help them remember the name. The parents announce the name, and explain its significance. When they are finished, everyone shouts the child's name three times, adding, "Be welcome!" Guests and witnesses come forward to offer gifts or to lay hands on the child in blessing. . . . When they have finished, the ritual becomes a party.

AGES 1 TO 10

First Flowering

T HE FIRST DESTINY RULES OUR LIVES from birth to the first
Saturn Return at around age twenty-eight, although it usually takes a few more years for fate to complete its movement
across the hinge and sort out the new destiny. So let us say that the
first flowering of our lives fills the years from birth to age thirty. But
in our culture, there is a social and psychological shift between the
growing years and adulthood at age twenty-one. The childhood years
create the foundations of our emotional, mental, and physical being.

What happens to us as infants and young children has repercus-
sions that extend throughout our lives. The mind retains everything,
and those impressions continue to inform, comfort, or disturb us.
Memories may remain buried until the first Saturn Return at age
twenty-eight or even the second in the late fifties, but eventually a
time will come for psychic housecleaning.

When we have grown strong enough to deal with them, memories
of pain or harm can be restored and healed. Some people do not

consciously remember childhood abuse until middle age. But it is not enough to understand the reason for our problems. The responsibility for healing is ours. Sometimes, by reliving the early stages of development, we can create a healthy childhood to replace the lost years. Childhood holds happy memories as well. Recovering these can help us to renew our love for life and tide us through later difficulties.

If you are a parent, you will find some useful clues to understanding your children in this analysis of the years from one to ten. But whether or not it is our fate to bear children, all of us still have a child within. Did your childhood include a year when everything went wrong? Why not take that birthday all over again? Can you identify a particularly happy year? Celebrate it once more. As you read about each year's challenges and celebrations, relive them. Nobody has a perfect childhood, but through memory we can recover the delight of those years that were successful and use adult understanding to fill in the gaps and heal unhappiness.

Celebrating Birthdays

WHEN PLANNING BIRTHDAY PARTIES for children, it is best to stay with the traditional format. Your child won't want to be teased because she seems "weird." Of course she is weird, and so are you—the word means "fate-full," and all of us interact with fate from the moment we are born.

No time is more "fate-full" than our birthdays. The instant of the first breath is the moment that engages our destiny with the cycles of the stars, the first important date in this lifetime. The second, of course, is the day on which we are born into the Otherworld through death. These are the dates that appear on our tombstones. They define our lives.

Children's birthdays are usually honored, but adults often prefer to skip their own. "Oh I didn't do anything much on my last birthday" is a response we saw on a number of our interviews. Don't blow off your birthday! Each birthday is a milestone on the journey between those two "births."

FATE DATES FOR AGES BIRTH TO 10		
Birth		All planets in natal position	•First Destiny begins
Age 2	♄ □ ♄	Saturn squares self	•Ego emerges
Ages 2, 4, 6, 8, 10	♂ ♂ ♂	Mars returns every two years	•Brings new energy
Age 7	♄ □ ♄	Saturn squares self	•Identity forms, sense of self is asserted

One

YEAR ONE IS A YEAR OF FIRSTS—culminating in the great milestone of the first birthday. In those first months, one of the most important senses is vision. Maturing vision shows us faces, sunshine and trees, food and toys, and all the wonders of the world. Sight is the door through which our brains gain access to the world, where we collect information to be processed later. We should remember the lesson of this year—first we see, then we understand and take action.

Other senses are developing as well. Bodily functions are being organized—the baby eats, sleeps, poos, pees, and coos. Crawling is an important prerequisite for developing neurological organization and coordination. Developmentally disabled children can sometimes be helped by relearning how to crawl.

By the first birthday, we have survived the dangers of infancy and laid the foundations for health and strength. Now that we are no longer dependent on others to interact with the world, the great adventure has begun.

THE BIRTHDAY

To celebrate your child's first birthday, get a cake that you will enjoy eating too and invite some friends—perhaps the sponsors who "adopted" the child at her naming ceremony. You didn't have one? You can take care of that any time during the child's first few years. She may even enjoy it more when she is a little older. When it's time for the cake, bring in the child, light the candle, and pass her from lap to lap, while singing the birthday song. One parent can make the wish, and the other can blow out the candle.

On the evening of the next full moon, take your child outdoors and hold her up so that she is bathed in moonlight. Give her the moon's blessing:

(Name), be blessed, little soul,
May you be wealthy, wise, and whole
With blessings of the holy three,
As I will, so mote it be....

Two

WITH THIS BIRTHDAY, MARS RETURNS to his natal position for the first time. This will happen every two years. With him comes a fresh wave of energy with which to begin a new cycle. Of course, with a two-year-old, energy is part of the lifestyle.

In the second year, the child is exploring the potential of her new abilities. If she can grasp, she can also throw. She can complete an action and is beginning to communicate with words. By the second birthday, she is a toddler. Now the child not only can see what she wants, she can go after it. The two-year-old learns how to use her body, tell the difference between herself and the world. Those new muscles demand action. During the first three years of life the brain is developing rapidly, so mental exercise is as important as physical.

This is a time of high risk, as the two-year-old has now achieved enough mobility and coordination to run quickly into danger. The street, a hot stove, sharp corners, ditches, and drops all seem to exercise a magnetic appeal. During the toddler years you cannot leave your child unwatched at any time. Every second is crucial to safety. The second birthday ought to be celebrated as a triumph of survival.

But the two-year-old is still close to the world of the angels, those old no-longer-embodied friends who visit in dreams. At two, we are beautiful, innocent of pretension. If we don't like something, we let the world know, even if it's not productive. The two-year-old has a primal authenticity. But at two we are terminally cute—Nature's way to ensure we will survive.

THE BIRTHDAY

The pattern for the second birthday can be the same as for the first, except that instead of passing the child around, you may want to leave her firmly strapped into her high chair. You will be aware by now that two-year-olds like to experience their food in every possible way, so protect the table and the floor.

Enjoy the steady light of the candles—they represent the life force that burns within. Make them red, for the energy of Mars. But the purpose of a life is to be lived, and the purpose of a cake is to be eaten, so once the candles are blown out, let your toddler attack her piece of cake at will!

Ask for the protection of Mars on all that incoming energy and ambition by calling on Ares himself or Athena, or Michael the Warrior Angel, to watch over your child and help her to channel aggressive energy productively.

Three

IT IS NOT UNTIL AROUND AGE THREE that most children can communicate well enough to reveal much about the spirit within. If vision enables us to take information in, then it is speech that allows us to get our insights and ideas out into the world. A child whose first speech is ignored will always wonder if she is worth listening to. Parents must be extra-patient with the three-year-old, for the self-esteem developed at this time is the foundation of a healthy personality. If you give toddlers love and attention they will blossom.

Without speech, it is much harder to demonstrate intelligence—it is not by chance that the speechless person is called "dumb." Listen to the toddler's garbled speech, her fascinated repetitions of new sounds, the silly stuff. If you are only pretending, the child will know. Listening is a form of love. Children will learn how to speak from what they hear—if you speak to them with courtesy, they will learn to do the same. Reading is another way to expand a child's mental universe. A book preserves the thoughts of someone the child will most likely never see—books show a child how to link minds with others, and open the way to a wider world.

With speech, we can learn to bless and pray. A simple "God or Goddess bless"—at bedtime, or a "Thank you" to the plants and animals that provide our food at a meal begin a habit of reverence for life, which is the foundation for a healthy spirituality.

THE BIRTHDAY

At the party for the third birthday, ask the child if she remembers anything about a life before, and what her purpose in this life is going to be. When you ask good questions of a three-year-old, you can get cosmic answers.

With the third birthday, you can begin the practice of lighting an extra candle for the coming year. As you do, say, "We thank God (or Goddess, or the spirits) for the lucky year that's already on the way!"

Your child will already be learning to recognize the song "Happy Birthday." By now it's almost universal. Z comments that she has heard it sung in Hungarian, in German, and in Spanish. Once again, Americans, the great culture makers, have come up with a song to fit what has become a worldwide custom.

Four

BY AGE FOUR WE CAN SEE THE EMERGING form of the child. Preferences and talents are beginning to emerge. Alice likes pink and is demonstrating excellent hand-eye coordination in her drawing.

Rory, on the other hand, can identify and pronounce correctly the names of all the dinosaurs. At this age, children are developing preferences in food, in TV, in the stories they want to hear. Parents and caregivers can aid them to develop by presenting a variety of options.

One set of characteristics that is beginning to be quite apparent is gender identity. While cultural expectations have some effect on this, innate preferences are even more important. No matter how hard parents may try to avoid imposing traditional gender roles, some boys will gravitate inexorably toward toy cars and tools, while some girls will show a definite preference for frilly pink clothing and dolls. Of course, most children display a mixture of characteristics and fall somewhere between these extremes.

This is a great time to develop the imagination. Play is a way to share ideas and emotions with others, with or without speech. The imagination is a mighty power. At the age of four, Diana was inventing stories that she dictated to her mother and then illustrated. Her granddaughter Arael drew pictures of families and explained all the relationships.

At four, the child is sufficiently aware of the difference between herself and others to appreciate playmates, both people and the toys to which she gives life through her imagination, and her "invisible friends." Treat these incorporeal beings with respect. Most of the time the child is aware at some level that these playmates are imaginary projections. "Going along" with the fantasy will help her to develop her imagination.

However, some children of this age actually do see ghosts, elemental spirits, and other beings. When adults ridicule or deny the child's perception, she learns to suppress it. If you think this is happening, talk with your child and make sure that what she is seeing is friendly. Gently let her know that not everyone can see these beings, and that it is best not to talk about them to people who won't understand. Teach your child to call on a guardian angel or spirit for protection.

By this time, many four-year-olds are attending nursery school or playgroups. Now they begin to bond with others of their own generation. These other children will be their contemporaries, the consumers of the products they will sell or create when they are grown. By sharing early experiences, a child becomes part of her generation's culture.

THE BIRTHDAY

By your child's fourth birthday, she will be enjoying the company of other children, and you may feel willing to face a children's birthday party. But keep it small. Try inviting one child for each year of the birthday girl's age.

When the birthday cake is brought in, ask, "How many candles are on your cake?" If the guest children are old enough, each can count off a number. If not, point to each child and say, "One, two, . . ." and so on. When you reach the child's age, add, "And one to bless the coming year! Now, make a wish, and blow!"

Five

THE FIVE-YEAR-OLD IS READY FOR SOCIETY'S first rite of passage, beginning kindergarten. At five, you have it all together. You can use the toilet, say "Thank you" for presents, you know who to be nice to and who you can ignore. For the first time, you are cool. At five, you are a pragmatist who defines things by what they are good for. You know what you like. At five, Diana's twin grandchildren have developed very distinct personalities. Michael says his favorite things are playing computer games. The big excitement in his life is getting his first pair of glasses. Arael says the most exciting thing she has learned this year is reading. Her favorite thing is playing with her friends. Her favorite color used to be pink, but now she likes the whole rainbow.

The first days of school may be traumatic as the reality of separation from home and family sinks in. This is the first of a series of detachments that will eventually leave you out on your own. But in general, five is an easy age. The school-age child has a "job." The increasing social awareness means that emotional relationships are more important. For some five-year-olds, being called "bad" is worse than a spanking.

By the time a child reaches school age, if not before, many parents have had to go back to work, and the child is being taken care of by others. The young child is aware of the pleasure her own body can give, but is also vulnerable to abuse by other people. It is the responsibility of the parent to make sure she is not victimized. Check out caregivers carefully. Get your child to talk about what is happening at day care or school. Make sure he understands what kind of touching is appropriate. A child who has been given enough love not to be emotionally needy, and whose integrity has been respected, will have the confidence to say "No."

If revisiting childhood memories brings back an awareness of abuse, the adult you are now can do the same for the child within. It was not your "fault." You do not have to submit in order to get the love you need. You are a complete and perfect person. This is a lot to take on alone—to get professional therapy for a time is not an admission of failure, but an intelligent adult response.

THE BIRTHDAY

Celebrate the fifth birthday by honoring your child's entry into this wider world. In addition to inviting five other children to the birthday party, take them all to a play park or zoo. (Don't try this alone! Recruit other parents or the child's sponsors!)

Put five candles on the cake in the form of a five-pointed star. When you light the one in the lower right-hand corner, say, "Blessed be your body." Next light the one in the upper left-hand corner, and say, "Blessed be your words." Light the upper right-hand candle and say, "Blessed be your energy." With the lower left candle, say, "Blessed be your feelings." Now move up to the top candle and light it, saying, "Blessed be your spirit."

Six

SUDDENLY THE SIMPLE WORLD of the five-year-old has become more complex. At six, we can see both sides of a question, and may be torn between choices. The six-year-old pushes the envelope emotionally, intellectually, and physically, and the wise parent sets clear boundaries.

At six, you can not only express your will but try to impose it on others, even grown-ups. You explore your powers, discovering what a good temper tantrum or guilt trip will do. It's therefore a crucial moment in parental development as well. The wrong reaction can stunt the child's personality or create a monster. The six-year-old is a natural actor and can explore behavior and options through dramatic play.

Now is a good time to start reading stories from books of mythology, especially those stories that show strong goddesses as well as gods. If you read your child Bible stories, be sure to tell those in which women as well as men take important roles. Give your children role models that are different from what they are getting from comic books and television.

The line between lying and innocent fantasy is sometimes hard to draw. Ally comes up with amazing explanations for how the milk got onto the floor. Sara protests she didn't touch the scribbled-on tax form, forgetting she has written her name there. The six-year-old can hide his feelings, or try to pass the blame on to others. A six-year-old is strong enough to hurt others. Now, when your child is first aware of moral choices, parents, teachers, and caregivers must nurture an awareness of the difference between right and wrong without instilling a sense of guilt.

But six can also be a time of developing friendships. First friendships are based on shared experience. Your best friend in first grade may not be your lifetime buddy, but that friendship will create in your heart a space for future relationships. Emotions develop as well. Crushes are fun—they make your heart flutter, and they are something precious that belongs to you alone. Love at six is at its purest and most divine.

When Z was a child, she was placed for a while in a convent school. Here is her story:

> When I was very small, I had to learn how to survive in a nun-nery. That first year it was alien to me. I hated the early rising, the incessant prayers, and I was hungry all the time. Then I fig-ured out how to charm the nuns and make them my allies. I had my first girlfriend, Eva, a blonde elfish girl who was very rebel-lious, but lacked the skill to hide her feelings. I loved her for this. She was in trouble a lot, and she needed me.
>
> But it was her eighteen-year-old older sister, Ruth, who was my first real love. I don't think that Ruth ever realized how I felt about her. I became a love addict for a while. The best friend with whom I played and the sister I adored from afar were sisters, part of the same thing.
>
> My imagination also focused on the nuns. The nuns who took care of the younger girls were young, in their twenties, I think. My two favorites were called Sister Gabrielle and Sister Jozafine. It was Jozafine who invited me to sing in the choir. This was a privilege. In choir, I lifted my small voice for the first time in song with my peers. I had been accepted into a tribe—I was part of a family greater than my broken home. The music was glorious, incense rose in generous pagan amounts, and we swayed under its spell.
>
> Surely the figure above the altar was the Queen of Heaven, surrounded by the fragrance of the Divine. The incense burner swung like a bell from the vault of the ceiling. It whooshed over-head like a great golden bird, spreading blessings of frankin-cense and myrrh. We prayed to the Virgin Mary before her many statues in the forest, the dormitory, the yard. We were encour-aged to build our own altars to her. We chanted splendid poems about the glory of the Mother of God, Immaculate Heart, the Rose of Heaven. Learning to love the Lady as the Virgin Mary prepared me to love the Goddess in all Her forms later on, as my feelings for Ruth and Eva prepared me to love other people.

THE BIRTHDAY

A birthday party for the six-year-old should be carefully planned, with a clear focus and not too many options. If other children are invited, make sure there are party gifts for each one. This helps to teach your child generosity, and gives the others something to play with while the birthday girl is reveling in her own. By now your child is probably already a fan of *Winnie the Pooh,* and will enjoy the rest of A. A. Milne's poetry. Get a copy of *Now We Are Six* and read the title poem at the party.

Seven

AT SEVEN, THE EGO EMERGES in its first plumage. That's what you need to get along in the world. Without ego, other people will define who and what you are. But everybody's ego wants to dominate, and a large part of maturity is learning cooperation instead of conflict. A thwarted ego may hate those who oppose it. Fortunately, at seven, today you may love the ones you hated yesterday. If children don't learn how to balance their own ego needs with those of others, or if they grow up in an environment in which hatred is the only defense they have, it may become a habitual response to the world. In time, whole generations may become conditioned to hatred, poisoning the future for *their* children.

For the seven-year-old, the task is to integrate this new self-awareness into the fabric of her personality. Both boys and girls need to develop this awareness. In the past, female children were conditioned to subordinate their egos to men. Fortunately this situation has been improving since the beginning of the twentieth century, even though progress sometimes seems to move two steps forward and one step back. Since the women's liberation movement in the 1970s, female role models have multiplied—even Barbie dolls have professions now! Choose books, movies, and toys that will support the concept of gender equality.

The first seven years are crucial to character as well as physical development. Ignatius Loyola, the founder of the Jesuits, believed that if you gave him a child to train up to the age of seven, it wouldn't matter who had him afterward. At age seven, all these early influences are being integrated. At seven years, Saturn is square to its natal position, a position of internal conflict that pushes us to detach from the collective unconscious and become a distinct individual.

Diana's grandson Evan, for instance, says he is really enjoying being in the second grade. The most exciting thing he's learned has been long division. The most fun he's had lately is hunting Easter eggs. His favorite things to do include writing to his pen pal and listening to stories such as *The Hitchhiker's Guide to the Galaxy,* the Harry Potter books, and *The Lord of the Rings.* At this time, some children will turn an interest into a passion, like Angie Miech, who started selling her little stuffed horse heads on sticks and eventually made enough money to buy a real horse.

Seven is a magical time, when many children have psychic experiences. In Catholic communities, this is the age when children are considered mature enough to become full communicants of the Church, a major milestone. Whatever the religion of the family, now is the time to begin including the child as a full participant. If you practice a nontraditional form of spirituality, explain to your child about freedom of religion and make sure she does not feel uneasy because you don't go to the same church as her friends. Discuss your beliefs and how you came to them. Encourage her to make her own decisions about religion while welcoming her to participate in yours.

THE BIRTHDAY

The seventh birthday opens this year of transformation. Take this opportunity to have a magical birthday celebration just for you, your child, and your partner. Pack up an exquisite picnic basket full of her favorite foods and take it to eat under a big old tree. You can go to a park or your own backyard. The tree can be an oak or a eucalyptus, a maple or a walnut. It doesn't matter so long as the tree is old, alive, and healthy. In addition to the picnic, bring a bottle of water, a bag of birdseed, and some pure incense.

Before you eat, sit down under the tree and quietly listen. Let the thoughts that come into your head arise and then float away. Encourage your seven-year-old to really listen to the wind in the leaves and the faint groaning sounds as the tree sways in the wind. These are the voice of the tree. What does she have to say?

When you have sat for a while, get up again and take your child's hand. Make a prayer to the tree with this poem, or find words of your own.

> *Tree of Life, so strong and tall,*
> *Past and future, you see all.*
> *Let (name) now your blessing win—*
> *Let him/her hear your voice within.*
> *With power of earth help her/him to grow,*
> *And at her/his back may fair winds blow.*
> *May sunfire burn away all pain,*
> *And good luck shower down like rain.*
> *Tree of Life, your blessing give,*
> *As long as you, this child shall live!*

Water the tree from your bottle, scatter the birdseed, and light the incense. Then take out your picnic and feast together.

Eight

DURING THE EIGHTH YEAR, we hone our responses to the world. By now we understand the customs and beliefs at home. It is school and its new social demands that are the challenge now. This is one of the years when Mars is passing through its natal position, bringing plenty of energy.

At eight, we become acutely aware of what it means in our culture to be a boy or a girl. Boys, especially, are likely to define themselves as "not-girls" and pointedly exclude girls from their clubs. Alex is full of plans to build a tree house, but doesn't want his sister to have anything to do with it. Girls may find this frustrating or confusing, as they are more likely to take their identity as given without making a big deal out of it. The genders play separately. This may be hard for a girl, whose identity does not depend on hating boys. Annie has a crush on a boy in her class, and comes home crying because the only way he knows to respond is to tease her.

The way to ease these social transitions is to develop other interests. Fortunately eight-year-olds are expanding their understanding of the world, and they are fascinated by the causes of things. What's inside the body? How does a seed turn into a tree? Not only gender awareness, but a sense of ethnic and national identity is developing now. This can translate into an interest in different spiritualities. Take your child to attend services of different religions and discuss what they believe and how this affects the way they act and look at the world. This is a good age for after-school classes, or sports activities. If the family travels, the eight-year-old wants to know about the similarities and the differences between children here and at home.

Eight-year-olds can appreciate the classic children's stories and, especially if you have been reading to them since babyhood, you will find that sharing your own favorites recaptures their magic for you as well. Continue reading tales from mythology—you can use them as a springboard for discussion of different cultures and beliefs. Films such as *Star Wars* are also great favorites and an inspiration for Hallowe'en costumes and dramatic play.

THE BIRTHDAY

The years from eight through the beginning of puberty are good times for "theme" birthday parties. A "Winnie-the-Pooh" birthday with "Pin-the-tail-on-the-Eeyore" as one of the games, or a "Star Wars" party with milk that you turn blue with a little food coloring and convince the children came from your pet Bantha will be remembered for a long time. Or, try a party in which each child wears a costume from a different country, and you serve different kinds of ethnic food.

Nine

AT NINE, WE MOVE INTO THE THRESHOLD space between childhood and puberty. In some communities, this shift is recognized by transferring children from elementary to middle school, although in others elementary school lasts through grade six. They are "Big Kids" now. Growth spurts lengthen arms and legs. Nine-year-olds are still children, but both we and they can see the promise of adolescence.

By now, tastes and interests are becoming clear. Lucy, who is horse-mad, comes home from school and sits down to draw them for an hour or two every day. The enthusiasms of later childhood are all encompassing; we may never know as much detail about any subject again. At nine, we are self-motivated, and can focus on a project for hours at a time. We love contests, get serious about sports, but begin to develop our inward life as well. We invent imaginary worlds, keep diaries, compose songs.

For many, the passion that will dominate our lives is beginning to emerge. You can guess who the young scientists will be, who has the potential to become a writer, an artist, a teacher. If a child does not have an interest already, parents should make an effort to help her find one. Not only is it good preparation for the future, but developing other interests will help balance the preoccupation with sex that comes when puberty kicks in.

Late childhood is a time when the spirit expands. This is one of Diana's memories:

> When I was growing up I had long conversations with the moon. Sometimes after dark, when I was supposed to be asleep, I would climb the ladder we kept so we could retrieve the volleyball from the flat roof of our house and sit there to gaze at the sky.
>
> I knew that the moon was a goddess. Because I was named after the Roman goddess of the moon, I had started reading mythology books at an early age. But when I sat gazing at that pure silver sphere I wasn't thinking of the old stories. It was the

magical energy of the moon that held me spellbound. I suppose my mother, who was a light sleeper, knew what I was doing, though I didn't realize it at the time, but she was wise enough to give me that freedom. Those cool, silver hours taught me stillness, taught me to open my awareness to the world around me, gave me peace.

I think now that parents who try to fill every hour of their children's lives with sports or study or social life are making a mistake. Children need those empty hours, lying in the grass and watching the play of light on leaves, or sitting wrapped in a blanket to look at the moon, to let the spirit grow.

THE BIRTHDAY

This is a time to have a birthday party "just for girls." Try a slumber party on the next weekend when there is a new moon (anywhere from the first thin crescent to half-moon size).

If your daughter's bedroom is not big enough, clear out the living or family room and decorate it in your child's favorite colors. Make sure she has some new pajamas to wear. Make a cake in the shape of a crescent moon and decorate it with the nine candles. Take the girls outside to look at the moon. Then go back inside, light the candles, and go on with the party.

Artemis, who in ancient Greece was the goddess of the moon, was also the protector of both young girls and boys. Boys may also enjoy a little moon-watching. Both boys and girls may be interested in the scientific as well as the magical aspects of the silver planet.

Ten

THE FIRST DECADE OF LIFE has seen us grow into developed individuals, big and strong enough to survive, in extremity, on our own. In earlier times, ten-year-olds were apprenticed to learn a trade or were helping their parents in the work of the shop or farm. Older siblings, especially girls, took responsibility for younger ones while the parents worked. Today, ten-year-olds may be considered responsible enough to do limited baby-sitting, and should certainly be expected to do household chores. Future trades are no longer decided in childhood, but at ten, we are fascinated by different jobs and fantasize romantic careers. "I'm going to be an astronaut," says Jamie. "I'm going to be a doctor and get married and have three children," says Lynn, and chooses their names.

Superheroes are still popular, filling the niche occupied by mythic heroes long ago. Children may admire leaders about whom they've learned in school, such as Martin Luther King Jr. Those who have grown up with a strong spiritual tradition dream of Bible heroes or goddesses and gods. This freedom to choose is precious. What the ten-year-old doesn't know is that the identity she chooses as an adult will not be permanent. We will need the ten-year-old's ability to reinvent ourselves and choose again.

Although sexual awareness and physical development vary widely, at ten we usually know where babies come from, even if it's hard to imagine why anyone would *want* to do such a thing. The facts about menstruation should be made clear, since a few girls have already started their periods, and more will begin soon. There is currently a growing concern over the fact that many are getting their first blood very early. Factors ranging from childhood obesity to the presence of added growth hormones in milk and meat have been blamed. Whatever the reason, this sign of physical maturity may now appear well before the girl is psychologically or socially ready to deal with its implications. If menstruation does begin, it should be treated in a calm, matter-of-fact manner.

Now is also the time to emphasize the need for healthy eating habits and exercise. Cultural conditioning regarding body type can have a devastating effect, both on boys who are taught to expect an impossible ideal and girls who fear they will be doomed if they don't attain it. It is hard to know how to counteract the influence of the media. Controlling access to television may help, as may widening exposure to the art of other times and cultures. It is equally important to supervise diet and exercise. Girls who don't support sports activity with a well-balanced diet may stay thin, but physical stress without proper nutrition may lead to osteoporosis by the time they are thirty. Adults who have body image issues may trace them back to these late childhood experiences.

At ten, the images of a popular boy or girl are well developed. Both genders form cliques, which often define themselves by who is excluded. What most ten-year-olds rarely realize is that everybody has insecurities. The "popular" kids who lead the cliques fear to lose their status, while their followers are afraid of falling out of favor.

In some ways, the child who is already considered a nerd has the advantage. Painful as social ostracism may be, the outsider is forced to develop her own resources, and has a head start on preparing for a career. At ten, Loren is so good with computers she can help fix her father's after a crash, and John is already filling notebooks with his novel. Whichever category your ten-year-old falls into, expanding her horizons by exposure to a variety of role models will be helpful. There are numerous books for this age group whose spunky heroines will show your child that she is not alone.

THE BIRTHDAY

The tenth birthday is a milestone. Not only has the first decade been successfully passed, but this age is in many ways the high point of childhood. Between now and the official entry to adolescence at thirteen, puberty will begin to loom with increasing intensity. Celebrate the person your child is now, for changes will be coming soon. The tenth birthday may be celebrated by a change such as allowing a new privilege or redecorating the child's room.

Organizations such as the Girl and Boy Scouts or Campfire include initiatory celebrations to mark achievements that may take place about this time. In ancient Greece, little girls of this age lived in the Temple of Artemis for a time, learning to serve the goddess of maidens. They were called the "little bears," and performed the Bear Dance for the goddess at her festival, the Brauronia. If your daughter has other friends whose families are sympathetic to women's spirituality, get a group of girls together to learn about the goddess Artemis and dance the dance of the Little Bears, dressed in saffron shifts.

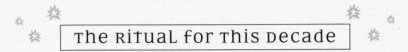

THE DREAMQUEST

This ritual has three parts. In the first, which may take place at any time before the quest, the child is encouraged to go through her collection of toys and set aside those which she has outgrown, to be given to charity or passed on to younger siblings or friends. Before doing so, set the toys to be given up in a circle around a candle. Ask the child to talk to and about each toy, with questions such as:

> "Does the toy have a name?"
>
> "Do you remember when you got it?"
>
> "What are some of your memories about playing with it?"

Some of the toys will be old and dear friends, while others may have been ignored and are easily given up. In some cases, the child may decide she wants to keep the toy after all. When all the toys have been honored, ask the child to say good-bye to each one, and bless it for the new owners, whoever they may be. Then have her blow the candle out and put the toys into bags to be taken away.

The second part of the process is the dream-vigil. Depending on the season and the setting, this can take place in a tent in the backyard, in a newly cleaned and/or decorated bedroom, or by making a sacred space in another room. If indoors, set candles in safe containers around the room, and play soothing music.

At bedtime, escort the child to the prepared space and put her to bed. Before you leave, say together the following prayer:

> *Toys with which I used to play*
> *I have outgrown and put away.*

AGES 1 TO 10 ❈ *First Flowering*

Good spirit come and be my friend,
And in my dreams a blessing send....

Leave paper and pencil by the bed, so that if the child has a dream she can remember, as soon as she wakes she can write it down. Take time to talk about the dream or any thoughts that occurred as she was waiting to fall asleep. Consider the content of the dream and discuss whether any of the figures in it might be spirit friends who will guard and help her in the future. Animals are particularly valuable allies. Encourage her to draw pictures of the figures or scenes she saw.

As the third part of the ritual, the dream-vigil can be followed, on the next day or later, by a traditional party at which new toys are given to replace the old.

NOTE: If you, as an adult, are working through old issues and reclaiming your childhood, you can perform a variation on this ritual in which you first remember and honor the toys you loved and then formally let them go. Then, hold your own vigil and seek a new spirit friend.

AGES 11 TO 20

It Was the Best of Times, It Was the Worst of Times

CHILDHOOD MEMORIES MAY BE HAZY, but most of us remember adolescence, those years of terror and wonder, only too well. In the space of ten years, our shapes and sizes, our minds, and our emotions all change. The unformed body of the child becomes that of a woman. Basic education is completed, although we will continue to learn lifelong. We cease to depend on our parents for support and protection, and begin to protect and support others.

The teens are a time of transformation. From the moment when the hormones of puberty kick in, we will be on a physical and emotional roller-coaster. Not until the changes of menopause that bracket our years of fertility will we again experience such extremes of anguish and joy. The biological imperatives of status and sex dominate adolescence. In this time of desires and dreams we find our first mission and shape our First Destiny. How can we guide our children through this troubled time? How can we heal our own memories?

Although adolescence is a time of continuing change, each child's development will be different. The yearly summaries should be taken as averages—what one child is like at thirteen will be true of another at fourteen, and one precocious fifteen-year-old may have characteristics that will not appear in another until two years later.

FATE DATES FOR AGES 11 TO 20			
Ages 12–14	♃ ☌ ♃	First Jupiter Return	•Hormones kick in •Personality asserts self
Ages 14–15	♄ ☍ ♄	Saturn opposes self	•Interest in sex picks up •Child asserts independence
Age 18	☊ ☋	Moon nodes return	•Emotions mature •Glimpses nature of First Destiny
Ages 18–21	♄ △ ♄	Saturn trines self	•Sense of vocation develops •Young adult separates from parents

Eleven

THE ELEVEN-YEAR-OLD IS A "pre-teen," still in many ways a child, but shadowed by oncoming adolescence. This used to be a rather "in between" age, but since the Harry Potter books burst on the scene, the eleventh birthday has become a major passage. In the traditional British boarding school system, this is the age at which students move from the lower to the upper school. It is on his eleventh birthday that Harry Potter is finally able to escape his dreadful aunt and uncle and begin a new life at the Hogwarts Academy of Witchcraft and Wizardry. He is only a First Year student, but for the first time he is free to make friends of his own and to discover his unique abilities.

The Harry Potter books appeal to everybody. Harry and his friends Hermione and Ron are good role models. They are not the most attractive or brightest or even the most popular kids in school, but they have the determination, cooperation, and compassion to triumph as well as survive. Grown-ups who read the books can, in imagination, make a new beginning as well. Many of us feel as if we were raised by Muggles (people without magic). Since we first became aware of our own individuality we have been looking for our "real" families and peers.

At eleven, on the verge of the hormonal explosion, imagination sets us free. This new growth may take the form of apparently ceaseless appetite and activity. Recognize your daughter's increasing independence and ability. Teach her your own kind of wizardry, and make sure she knows she is just as marvelous as Harry Potter in your eyes.

THE BIRTHDAY

If your eleven-year-old is a fan of the books, give him or her a Harry Potter birthday party. Eleven-year-olds are on the threshold of the age of magic. For presents, give magical things. Decorate with pictures from the book or movie, and make a hat and robe. Present your child with a letter of invitation to Hogwarts School of Witchcraft and Wizardry. Get onto the Harry Potter Web site and let the Sorting Hat assign each party guest into one of the Houses.

Twelve

IN OUR TWELFTH YEAR, Jupiter returns for the first time to his position in our birth charts. Since this is also the year for Mars to swing through once more, this will be an age of expansion, when one is eager for adventure. But if the eleventh year was at times tumultuous, the girl of twelve is often perceptibly more mature. For the twelve-year-old, even parents can be appreciated as companions. Friendships formed at this age may last a lifetime. Hurt a child at this age and you may find she will be back to get even a decade later. These are no longer children, but people in their own right, with a very sensitive integrity. They want respect, and if you don't give it, you will not get any back.

At twelve-and-a-half, Saturn is just past his opposition in a quincunx position, heralding a physical growth spurt and increasing body awareness. Although boys and girls of this age are for the most part still separate species, girls may be starting to imagine romance, usually with safely distant figures such as rock stars or media personalities. Other girls this age are still fixated on horses, whose strength and beauty hold out the promise of companionship with an alien power that can bring fulfillment and freedom.

Diana recalls her own youthful love affair with horses:

> It lasted until I had a horse of my own. Dealing with the reality of cleaning stalls and grooming, and the struggle to get cooperation from a stubborn, willful creature of limited intelligence taught me a lot about the difference between romance and reality. The relationship was rewarding, but it took work. When, years later, I saw the film of The Black Stallion, I realized this was the idealized portrayal of what I had believed horses to be. Later it occurred to me that many women go through a similar evolution of feeling with regard to men!

Twelve is the median age for girls to begin menstruation. Some will have started already, others will begin in the following year or two. At twelve, however, a girl is beginning to look like a woman, and though she may tower over boys her own age, she is old enough to be preyed on by older boys, and to move into a social setting in which she may be pressured into sex and risk pregnancy. It is imperative that parents pay attention to their daughter's development, and if there is any chance at all that she may become sexually active, make sure she understands how and why she should be protected.

If you have got your kids focused at an earlier age on some activity that engages their creative instincts, the increasing energy of adolescence can be channeled into it rather than fixating on sexual competition. You can still try to divert that energy, by creating adventures, camping, or travel, though it will be more difficult as time goes on.

THE BIRTHDAY

Use the twelfth birthday as an opportunity to celebrate this moment of equilibrium—it may be the last you will have for a long time!

Suggest spending this last birthday before the teens as a family party. Plan an expedition—a trip, or a dinner and movie, and let your birthday child navigate. Choose something that both parents and child will enjoy.

Thirteen

IN A CULTURE THAT IS VIVIDLY AWARE of numbers, the thirteenth birthday is a milestone—the official entry into the teens. At thirteen, young people are expected to deal with multiple classes and teachers, and to work with less supervision on school projects and other activities. Thirteen is a time to bring mind and body into balance. It is the beginning of the separation from one's parents, peacefully, if they are understanding, or through rebellion. The teenager is beginning to find her own power.

At the beginning of the teens, children who have found a passion in later childhood are capable of great achievement, especially in sports such as figure skating, gymnastics, and swimming. Figure skaters Oksana Bayul and Tara Lipinski and gymnasts Olga Korbut and Nadia Comaneci were international stars at this age. Thirteen-year-old Elise Macmillan and her older brother Evan have a thriving business making barnyard animals out of chocolate.

The challenge will be to adjust to the changes and maintain the standard of excellence when other needs and desires begin to grow.

Physical separation from parents can be useful. These days, travel can help, spending summers away from home. If aunts or uncles are compatible, they can serve as foster parents against whom the teenager does not feel the need to rebel.

In some religious traditions thirteen-year-olds are welcomed into full participation in the community. Judaism offers the Bar or Bat

Mitzvah as an official opportunity for the child to demonstrate adult-level spiritual understanding.

For a girl, the first period, or the stabilization of the menstrual cycle, begins the transformation of puberty. For many cultures, a girl's first blood is a particularly sacred time. Among the Apaches, it is celebrated with a feast at which the girl undertakes tasks that will magically prepare her for a productive adulthood, and is then formally presented to the community.

In our culture, menarche can be honored in a variety of ways, from a family feast at which the girl is presented with red roses to a women's ritual involving the mother and members of the Goddess community.

Either way, the start of menstruation creates big changes. As Z puts it:

> Bleeding is hard to get used to when you used to be free of such surprises. There you are, playing soccer with the boys, and suddenly blood is flowing down your legs like a small river. What to do? You stop your childish games and go home, ashamed to realize that you must hide your blood or else be ridiculed. This is what happened to my mother, who was a tomboy. When I got my period at eleven, I came into the dining room where my parents were having dinner. My father was a doctor, so I pulled my panties down so that he could make sure I hadn't been injured. Mother quickly showed me how to use pads. But my bleeding continued so heavily that I couldn't go to school.
>
> This time off from school had to be filled, so I started reading my father's books. Many of the novels about grown-up relationships were over my head, but I became an avid reader, which changed my life because it helped me to become a writer.
>
> By the time I was thirteen my body had learned how to handle the cycle and I would stop bleeding after five days. I still had to plan my life around it, making sure I had the herbal teas, and being ready with excuses for things I wouldn't be able to do. "Only Women Bleed," goes the song. How true. And how oppressive. I didn't honor my bloods as later feminism has taught us to

do. It is hard to love something that makes you ache, dirties your
pants, restrains your movements, and if you are not careful,
smells!

   By the time I was thirteen I was a young woman. My cycle
was established, and I could keep it hidden. I fell in love with my
first boyfriend, whom I met on my summer vacation. He was five
years older—an older man. My mother talked to his parents and
he was removed from the city. Poor Bandi—deported for love! My
heart was broken. I didn't know until much later why he never
showed up again. The experience left me with the conviction that
boys/men were unreliable. I don't think I ever again loved so
deeply. Why give your heart away when it will only get broken?

THE BIRTHDAY

The official entry into the Teens should be honored by some recogni-
tion of a girl's new status. Take a deep breath and let her invite her
friends for a "Girls' Night Out." Since parents will still have to provide
the transportation, discreet chaperonage can be arranged. The girls
get to choose where they want to eat and where they want to go—a pizza
parlor and the ice rink, a rock concert or a movie. Make sure your
daughter understands that she needs to live up to your trust in her.

Fourteen

FOURTEEN IS A YEAR OF CONVERGENCE. We complete our second
Jupiter Return, a sign of expansion when one wants to test the
boundaries. However this year will also see Saturn moving into opposition to his natal position. When this happens, we become more aware
of ourselves in the context of the greater world around us. This may
create a sense of insecurity in the fourteen-year-old to whom it is happening for the first time.

   The fourteen-year-old is becoming more self-aware; identity is firm-
ing up and with it comes an increasing independence of thought. This

is dramatically revealed in the diary kept by Anne Frank while she and her family lived in hiding during the Nazi occupation of Holland. Her life was short, but her words reached the world.

The node change that Saturn goes through at this point creates great sensitivity to hypocrisy and a lack of tolerance for ambivalence. Parents, struggling with the complexities of their own lives, may find it difficult to deal with the fourteen-year-old's certainty.

The fourteen-year-old is also developing her own spirituality. Spirituality may take many forms. When Diana was this age, she read the Bible from cover to cover with great interest. Four girls who invoked goddesses for a Girl Scout Interfaith ceremony reported their experiences in *Blessed Bee,* a magazine for pagan families. The girl portraying Kuan Yin liked the energy of the bodhisattva because "she is nice and cares about others." The one who invoked Pele developed an ongoing relationship with the Hawaiian goddess. The girl who called the Yoruba orisha Yemaya felt that it was a demonstration of tolerance and equality, and the one who called Corn Mother was happy to teach the participants about Native American ways.

All four found a particular reward in the reaction of the younger girls present to the energy of these goddesses. As one said, "The little girls that were there welcomed us with open arms. They are young, but they know a lot more than you think." It is clear that the fourteen-year-old "priestesses" also learned something about making contact with Spirit and the power of the Goddess within.

Girls this age need to understand that boys are entering their time of fastest growth. They may begin to develop an interest in girls, but are not yet ready to admit it. Sexual drive is increasing. As male hormones flare, boys who formerly defined themselves as "not girls" may now define themselves as members of gangs and turn against each other. For girls, especially those who are socially precocious and involved with older boys, the pressures of sexuality are growing. At this age, our own responses may frighten us, and we don't know how far we should go. If we give boys what they want, our names may end up scrawled on bathroom walls. If we don't, we won't be "popular."

By the age of fourteen, when a girl's adult body type has emerged, issues relating to our bodies become important once more. Those who have curves feel they are too fat; those who are slim fear they are too thin. Breasts are too big or too small. Acne is a constant threat. It is a rare girl who can appreciate her own beauty at this age. Some diet and exercise to the point of anorexia, while others binge. Diana recalls how she used to gaze into the mirror, teasing her eyebrows to slant upward, until she realized that no matter what she did she was never going to look like Audrey Hepburn.

For some women, the battle with body image that begins now will continue lifelong. It can be a useful exercise to find a picture of that teenaged self and give it a good hard look. The girl in the picture is probably prettier than you remembered—she is certainly better looking than she ever believed at the time. Appreciate her unique beauty. Tell that younger self that she is lovely, not in the same way as a fashion model or movie star, but as the woman you now know she is destined to become.

Several recent books, such as Rachel Wiseman's *Odd Girl Out,* have focused on the problem of cliques among teenaged girls. While boys may be more likely to fight physically, girls, who are better at emotional intimacy, for the same reason are much better at emotional violence. In the search for identity, which is one of the major tasks of adolescence, one of the easiest, and least productive, ways to define oneself is by making distinctions between the "in-group" and those who are "other." The social ostracism that can destroy a teenager's life is part of the same pattern of behavior as sexism and racism. If we can teach our children to value their own unique individuality and fulfill their potential, they will be free to value that of others.

THE BIRTHDAY

This birthday is a good opportunity to give your daughter a gift that will help her to deal with issues relating to her size and shape. If she's worrying about baby fat, pay for her enrollment in a teen exercise program; if she's fixated on sports, steer her toward something relaxing.

Recruit your own friends to put on a Teen "Exploring Style" Party, where your daughter and her friends can experiment with makeup, have their colors done, and get advice on what looks good on different shapes. Obviously this has to be planned with sensitivity. If the girl is still fixated on horses, for instance, she'll be more interested in a new bridle than a new bra.

Fifteen

BY THE FIFTEENTH YEAR, Saturn has moved into opposition to its natal position in our charts, pushing us to separate our own values from those imposed by society. If parents have a consistent and balanced value system, the fifteen-year-old is less likely to revolt, but any sign of indecision is likely to provoke anger and rebellion.

In the Middle Ages, a girl of fifteen might be married and running her own household. A traditional ballad sings of the boy who was married at fourteen, a father at fifteen, and dead at sixteen. Today, a fifteen-year-old is less likely to be given so much responsibility, but some are ready to strike out on their own. Fifteen-year-old Erin Lely has organized her friends into a baby-sitting service. Josh DeFalco is so good with computers he's started a business repairing them.

The fifteenth year is a time of dreams and aspirations. For Z, it was a time of friendship and discovery:

> When I was fifteen years old I worked the hardest in school. The curriculum was demanding. I was learning languages. But more important, I was developing a lifelong friendship with Marcsi, who made me laugh and with whom I imagined my future. We shared a rare devotion. My heart was so full! The support Marcsi gave me as a writer, as a girl, as a student, as an "only" child, was magical. She was the sister I never had, the best friend I never had, my role model. Marcsi filled all my emotional emptiness. With her I had a holy alliance that healed my childhood hurts. She mirrored me back to myself in a loving light, never doubting me.

*Marcsi brought me food from home, shared her Tizorai, which
in Hungarian means the brown bag lunch. At ten A.M. I ate the
apples her mother had packed for her lunch. I had half her sand-
wiches and drinks. I don't know why I myself had nothing.
Mother cooked at night, but all I remember from my childhood,
when the horn of plenty was pointed toward my house, was
bread and milk and barack lekvar—apricot jam. I don't recall
taking them with me to school.*

*Fifteen was long and blurry even back then. A time of wait-
ing—for womanhood, waiting to be in love, waiting to be recognized. I remember waiting for my breasts to finish growing,
waiting for the school year to end, waiting to spend a last
summer with Marcsi on the Duna River in Visegrad.*

*At the age of fifteen I published my first short story and was
paid for it. I got a swelled head and vowed to become a screen-
writer and a humorist. I did become a writer, but it was not until
recently that I have resurrected the old but never forgotten dream
of writing for the movies.*

The fifteenth year can have tremendous meaning. At this time,
values are forming, dreams are being born. Adolescents give their loyalty to friends, to causes. We learn the difference between what is "out
there" and "in here." We must learn to respond to the world around us
while retaining our own sense of ethics. Venus rules this opposition of
Saturn to himself, bringing with her a concern for harmony. Emotional
and physical yearnings for love are for the first time connected.

In the confused world of adolescence, the search for identity may,
if not wisely guided, direct this energy into forming cliques based on
superficial values—appearance, sexual orientation, ethnicity, even
manners. Who's "in" and who's "out" shift with bewildering rapidity.
Girls' cliques are capable of an emotional violence as brutal, in its way,
as the physical violence of male gangs. If parents condone race hatred
or prejudice against those of different religions or sexual orientation,
hatred can become a substitute for positive values. The most dangerous fanatics are teenagers.

Some of these astrological configurations will not occur again until our mid-forties. The midlife crisis is prefigured by this adolescent tumult of emotion. This signals the birth of the great dream. What we dream at fifteen will demand manifestation, if not now, then in later life. These dreams become our destiny.

THE BIRTHDAY

This is a good year to repeat the Dreamquest ritual suggested for the tenth birthday, but this time it can be an adventure as well. In addition to whatever celebrations are scheduled with family or friends, take your child away for the weekend to some place of great natural beauty. Depending on the season or location, this could be a mother-daughter (or father-son) camping trip, or you can stay at a motel (you'll want separate rooms). Spend the day walking, and that night, let the girl sit out by the campfire or in her room with a candle. Ask the blessing of Artemis, who watches over maidens, and leave her to her meditations.

Sixteen

SWEET SIXTEEN AND NEVER BEEN KISSED? These days, it's unlikely. But this is the age at which sexual attraction is acquiring meaning. For the first half of this year, mother Venus will continue to rule, as she will once more when you reach forty-five. But love hurts more when you're sixteen. Youth doesn't yet know how to handle the pain and the desire. In the second part of the year, sexuality begins to involve the emotions as well as the hormones. The sixteen-year-old has to learn the ethics of the heart.

In the regular alternation of focus typical of the teenage years, the sixteen-year-old is looking outward once more. Identity is being challenged by the outside world. Inner values may have a new focus and strength. It is time to be assertive and make a mark upon the world.

At sixteen one is entitled to undergo our society's first adult rite of passage—learning to drive a car. Not all teenagers are ready for this challenge, but those who are get their first taste of adult mobility. It is up to parents to teach them to use this privilege wisely.

Young people at this age adapt easily to new environments, whether they are gangs or alternative families. Foreign travel is a good way to expose teenagers to new things. If we establish bonds with hospitable people we may make friends for life. Sometimes external circumstances offer dramatic opportunities.

When Z was sixteen, Hungary exploded in rebellion against the Soviet domination.

> *At this age, I left Budapest, my hometown. Everything I had learned in my first sixteen years told me that there was no future for me in Hungary, and now was my only chance to get out. The Iron Curtain had been there all my life, and after the Hungarian Revolution, it went back and stayed there for almost four decades.*
>
> *It was a bold move for a sixteen-year-old girl with no skills, not even a high school diploma. But the winds of fate were behind me, and I knew it. I made it across the border to Austria, and found refuge with a wonderful adoptive family in Innsbruck, where I finished school in a bilingual program. The Fates help those who help themselves. The helping hand is usually to be found at the end of your own wrist.*

THE BIRTHDAY

Another year brings another opportunity to recognize growth. This year, the birthday party may be co-ed. Chaperone discreetly—the point is to show your daughter that you trust her to keep things under control. A good birthday gift would be to let her travel alone to visit a relative or friend.

Seventeen

WITH THE SEVENTEENTH YEAR, the pressures of adulthood begin to loom on the horizon. Schoolwork is intense. Some may be graduating from high school at this age. Others are preparing to do so and planning for the tests they will need to pass to get into college. At this age, many are holding jobs during the summer or after school. Even unpaid work can be a good introduction to the adult world.

Emotions are also intensifying. We swim in the love of things, subjects, friends, and the world. At times the seventeen-year-old will enjoy playing like a child, but she has matured, and is ready for more responsibilities. She is less gullible and trusting, but still open to new experiences.

At this age one is also capable of great loyalty and devotion. This may take the form of loyalty to a group or cause, or religious enthusiasm. She may decide she wants to be a nun, or a witch. The seventeen-year-old wants to belong—to a gang, the "in-group" or the "weird group," a church or cult, an army. She wants to be accepted and needed, to be part of a larger family. Tests and challenges may be welcome.

At seventeen, opinions are held and expressed with great certainty. We take moral stands, and cannot understand why others, especially parents, feel the need for patience and compromise. We are eager to put our convictions into practice, and resent the efforts of adults to protect us. We want to walk the walk and live the dream. Parents may be startled when the philosophy of life they have been teaching suddenly becomes an outline for action, but the seventeen-year-old is tasting her power, ready to make her own mistakes and take the consequences.

As Lee puts it, "My daughter is almost grown at seventeen-and-a-half with a steady boyfriend and a part-time job. I hardly get to see her anymore. The transformation that I have witnessed since I bought her that first car is simply amazing. She has turned into a pleasant, responsible young adult right before my eyes."

THE BIRTHDAY

The new seventeen-year-old will want to plan her own birthday party, thank you. The most a parent can do is to offer suggestions. Find an opportunity to talk about last year's dreamwork. Do those results make more sense now? Does she still have the same dream? How does she visualize herself carrying out her plans five years from now?

Eighteen

BY THE TIME THE YEAR ENDS, most teens have finished their high school years and are entering the adult world. Depending on the time and place, we may be eligible to marry without parental permission, to vote, to join the military, or to be drafted. Some are starting college or professional training. Others already have jobs. Parents are no longer legally required to support us. Some eighteen-year-olds have children of their own, with or without marriage. But with adult rights comes adult legal status and responsibilities.

Between ages eighteen and twenty-one, Saturn trines Saturn and we come up with a working philosophy of life. Society challenges us to put our ideals into practice, and generally we are confident that we can take on that challenge. The meaning of this age is, "Create yourself, you have all the elements now!" The mind is hungry for connections, both social and geographical. A doorway is opening to a new world.

In the eighteenth year, the moon's node returns to its natal position. This configuration occurs every eighteen to nineteen years, and each time it signals a new stage in emotional maturation. This time, we may gain a glimpse of what the mission for the First Destiny will be. As new adults we are becoming able to handle the stresses and make the commitments of our new status.

THE BIRTHDAY

The eighteenth birthday marks a coming-of-age, a precursor to the full legal status that will come at twenty-one. Especially if your daughter is going out on her own or away to college, this is a good time to make a change in financial status. If she does not already have her own checking account, give her enough money to start one and teach her how to balance it. Talk about budgeting; share information on family finances so that she will have a more realistic idea about what it costs to live.

Nineteen

B Y THE NINETEENTH YEAR, the fertility cycle is well established. Hormones are up and running, and these days, when the mechanics of fertility are so well understood, it is the responsibility of both sexes to keep them under control. Boys are constantly horny. Girls are vulnerable to the compulsion to continue the species, the desire for motherhood.

At this age, we are beginning our mature, fertile years, which will last until menopause stops the biological clock. In earlier times, a high mortality rate pushed us to reproduce as soon as we were physically able. Today there is no danger that humans will die out. The challenge now is to control our drives and make the decision to have children wisely.

If the young person has had the misfortune to be abused as a child or teenager, this physical flowering may be warped. Abuse, neglect, or other negative or ambivalent experiences will make it hard for the victim to realize her positive physical and emotional potential. It is important, therefore, to try to work through these experiences and heal the wounds now.

From the physical point of view, the late teens and early twenties are the optimal time for motherhood. Bodies are strong and supple, and one has the stamina to wake up five times during the night to feed the baby and still function during the day. From the emotional and mental point of view it may be a different story.

Z remembers, "The young heart is full of species love and energy at this age. I should know—I was pregnant at age nineteen and a mother at twenty. I don't remember much about those years. By the time I was twenty-two I had two boys. I raised them, but I've repressed most of the memories. It had to be hard. . . ."

Despite the temptations, at this age most young people will put off parenthood. This is the time to take charge of our personal destiny. The young adult feels an increased sense of personal autonomy and the freedom to make life choices. Intellectually, this period can be very stimulating, especially if you are lucky enough to be able to travel or pursue your education. This is a time when many are eager to learn more about religious or spiritual ideas. The philosophy that will shape our lives is taking shape. The potential that was only glimpsed at fourteen is beginning to unfold. We can intuit our futures.

Diana recalls her college years:

> When I arrived at Mills College I felt as if I had come home. Their motto was "Unum destinatio, viae diversae—*One destination, many roads.*" For the first time, I didn't feel like a misfit. Whatever I wanted to do, I could usually find at least one other person who was interested in doing it with me. Because I was attending a women's college, I felt free to excel. At that point I was only vaguely aware of my own sexuality, but the school was small enough so that students and faculty could develop friendships, and the intellectual exchange was tremendously exciting. I made friends there who are dear to me to this day.

THE BIRTHDAY

At this point, you are no longer letting your parents plan your birthday parties, or if they do want a family celebration, you are probably also doing something else with your friends. On your nineteenth birthday, celebrate your newly matured body. Test your limits. If you enjoy the outdoors, take a long hike or go on a camping trip. At home or on the town, go out and dance!

Twenty

A T TWENTY YEARS OLD, we are out of our teens at last. By the time we get here, our bodies are fully formed, our hormonal cycles stabilized, and our emotions usually under control. We know it all—certainly more than our parents do. Sometimes we are even right.

At twenty we are devoted to causes, ready to throw our lives away because we cannot really believe that we might die. Our lives are shiny and new, not a worn-out garment we are trying to preserve. Later we will have time to celebrate what we have learned, but at twenty, we can hardly wait to apply everything we know.

Now is the time to articulate your goals and dreams. But beware of locking yourself into one role. Linger before you leap. Let the wisdom of your earlier years fill and guide you. After all, wisdom is common sense applied to living. You may think you know exactly what you are going to do with your life, but the one thing that is certain about life is change.

THE BIRTHDAY

Get ready to say good-bye to your teenage years. Invite everybody who has helped you along the way—your current best friends and old friends who've been out of touch. Invite teachers, relatives, all those who helped to shape the person you have become. Put twenty candles on your cake. As you blow each one out, name the age it represents, and try to remember something important from that year.

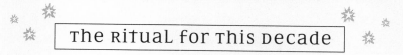

The Ritual for This Decade

THE WELCOME INTO WOMANHOOD

The transformation from child to adult is one of the most significant passages in our lives. For women, its beginning is marked by a visible physical event—the beginning of menstruation. This is a wonderful opportunity to get a girl started off right. Getting our first blood signals our potential to create the human race. Happy women start out with happy rituals.

This ritual can be performed at any time from first menstruation to the end of the teens, for a single person, or for several girls together. This is a ritual for women and girls only (if fathers and brothers want to congratulate her, they can arrange a family celebration at another time). If the candidate is a young girl and her mother is present, the following ritual should be completed as the first step in the passage.

The girl and her mother approach the tub or pool. Their wrists or waists are bound together with a red ribbon or cord. When they reach the tub, the mother turns to the daughter and tells her that this ribbon represents the cord through which her blood flowed to give life. But now she is becoming a woman, and it is time for her to walk alone. Is she willing to do so?

When the daughter says she is willing, the mother responds that she is willing to let her go, and cuts the ribbon.

Next comes the purification, which can be used to prepare candidates for this or other rites of passage. The length and nature of the purification should suit the ritual, the setting, and the season.

You can use a bathtub, a hot tub, a river, a lake, or the sea. If it is done in the tub, scent the water with bath oil, or float rose petals or fragrant herbs. Participants should be provided with towels, fresh robes, and seashells for dipping the water (those sold as baking shells work well).

The girl's friends help her to disrobe and enter the bath. If the pool or tub is large enough, several of them may also go in. They take the shells and pour water over her to cleanse her in body and spirit. Afterward, she can soak for a little while, meditating on the waters of the womb from which all life is born.

Her friends then help her to get out of the pool, dry her, and robe her in a new or clean garment, preferably white or red. She can also have a wreath of flowers.

The welcoming group should include women of all ages. Participants should be familiar with the structure and purpose of the ceremony, and should bring food and drink for the celebration and gifts for the candidate(s).

When the bath is finished, everyone forms a line beginning with the mother(s), if present, and ending with the daughter. The line moves to the entrance to the room where the ritual will take place. If the group is small, they can all have a group hug, but if there are more than four people, you can try the "passage embrace," which is like being carried through the birth passage once more.

Participants form two lines, facing each other, and each pair joins hands. The girl being initiated approaches, the first pair open their arms to admit her between them, then grasp hands again around her.

One says, "Through woman's womb you entered this world—"

The other woman replies. "Through women's arms you enter this circle—"

Then they release the girl to pass into the embrace of the next pair, who admit her with the same words, and so on until she has passed all the way through. Everyone then forms a circle. Any premenstrual girls who are present can wait until the others are all in place and then enter and sit outside the circle as observers.

When all are seated, the oldest woman present explains that they are gathered together to instruct the girl (or girls) in the mysteries of womanhood. She is formally seated on a decorated chair, and everyone applauds.

One of the most powerful archetypes in our culture is that of the Triple Goddess, associated with the new, full, and waning moon. To dramatize this, three women may speak the parts of the three faces of the Goddess (from chapter 2 of *Priestess of Avalon* by Marion Zimmer Bradley and Diana L. Paxson).

MAIDEN:

I am the flower that blooms on the bough.

I am the crescent that crowns the sky.

I am the sunlight that glitters on the wave

and the breeze that bends the new grass.

No man has ever possessed Me,

and yet I am the end of all desire.

Huntress and Holy Wisdom am I,

Spirit of Inspiration, and Lady of Flowers.

Look into the water and you will see My face mirrored there,

for you belong to Me....

MOTHER:

I am the fruit that swells on the branches.

I am the full moon that rules the sky....

I am the sun in her splendor,

and the warm wind that ripens the grain.

I give myself in my own times and seasons,

and bring forth abundance.

I am Mistress and Mother, I give birth and I devour.

I am the lover and the beloved,

and you will one day belong to Me....

CRONE:

I am the nut that clings to the leafless bough,

I am the waning moon whose sickle harvests the stars.

I am the setting sun

and the cool wind that heralds the darkness.

I am ripe with years and with wisdom;

I see all the secrets beyond the Veil.

I am Hag and Harvest Queen, Witch and Wisewoman,

and you will one day belong to Me....

Each woman in the circle talks about her own life experiences, especially those involved with puberty, leading to a general discussion. The focus should be appropriate to the needs of the girl—a discussion for a pubescent girl should concentrate on how to handle the awakening sexual awareness of adolescence and the nature and needs of boys and men, while a ceremony for a young woman would consider the responsibilities of love and children, or how to do without them.

When each woman has passed on her wisdom, she gives the girl a flower or a gift. The last gift should be a ring with a red stone, which the girl can then wear on the days when she is bleeding to celebrate her womanhood. After all the gifts and advice have been given, celebrate with food and drink.

AGES 21 TO 30

Brave New World

IN OUR TWENTIES, WE TAKE THE NEXT STEP, beginning to realize our potential, integrating the lessons of childhood and adolescence. Social and personal rituals help us to complete this transition. Legally, we attain full adult status, with the rights and the responsibilities that go with it. The twenties are also the time when we begin to make commitments. Will we choose to walk hand in hand with a partner or go it alone? Are we ready to commit to a career, or do we just want a job to keep us going while our "real lives" lie elsewhere? Our bodies are pushing us to use our fertility, but is this the right time?

We're grown-ups now, out on our own—or are we? For many, the first flight out of the nest is a short one. The cultural model of the first half of the twentieth century included an assumption that by the early twenties, education would be completed. Males were starting in entry-level jobs; females were getting married and starting families. Today, economic insecurity and high housing prices cause many twenties to return, at least for a time, to the parental nest. A longer life expectancy may diminish the pressure to be out and achieving. Now that our life spans are closer to those of hobbits, Tolkien's designation of this age as the "tweens, that irresponsible age between twenty and thirty..." takes on a new significance.

During the decade of our twenties, we conclude our First Destiny, completing the mission we've been working on since we were born. The first Saturn Return, which begins at age twenty-eight, is a hinge. By the time it has swung us around at about age thirty-two, we will be walking a path that is either new or redefined, depending on our experiences and the ways in which Saturn interacts with the other planets in our personal charts.

The reassessment that takes place during the first Saturn Return in essence says, "Here is your homework!" whereas the second Saturn Return will make us ask whether we have done it....

The twenties can bring many events and changes, not all of them the ones we expect. At the Goddess 3000 Festival, held every year in LaHonda, California, women work together according to age groups. The first consists of the "Maidens"—young women who have not yet passed through the first Saturn Return. The second age group is the Queens—women in the productive years between the first and second Saturn Returns, followed by the Crones, who are moving toward the third. Here is how Deborah, one of the participants, describes her experience:

> *As the destiny groups assembled in the field (to plan their contribution to the ritual), I hesitated to join the Maidens, not because it was the smallest group, nor because I was embarrassed by my youth. On the contrary—I was and always had been a person who kept older friends and older partners, not intentionally, but because my energy was usually drawn toward people with more maturity and experience than myself. For nearly twenty minutes I watched the large cluster of Queens (women in their forties and fifties), before I begrudgingly walked toward the Maidens' group, joining it after the round of introductions had already begun. My turn came.*

FATE DATES FOR AGES 21 TO 30

Ages 21–23	♅ □ ♅	Uranus squares self	•Possible identity conflicts
Age 22	♄ □ ♄	Saturn squares self	•Courage covers insecurity
			•Inner conflicts activated
			•Dynamic formative period
			•Initiation into responsibility
Age 24	♃ ☌ ♃	Jupiter Return	•Values and ethics solidify
			•Boundless energy
Ages 24–25	♄ ⚹ ♄	Saturn sextiles self	•Sex, friendship, commitment
			•First mission "peaks"
Ages 28–30	♄ ☌ ♄	First Saturn Return	•Shift from First to Second Destiny
			•Stressful period, suicide danger
			•Entry to full adulthood
			•Time to develop inner resources

"I want to be honest with you all," I sighed. "I am by age a member of this group, but I fear that I don't share connections with you. I am a stepmother and a committed partner, and have been so for years. I am a graduate student and a member of the workforce. How many of you are?"

The hands went up, and the discussion went deep. Wendy was a nurse. Cecilia had her own children. Jessica taught college classes in Women's Spirituality. Even the youngest were not girls—they were young women with serious goals, accomplishments, and responsibilities like mine. I was surprised, and I learned a great lesson that had been in my heart for years but hadn't surfaced: to be youthful is to have wisdom and power akin to the first single flame fighting with its blue glow against the cold.

*At the ritual, we all contributed poetry and wisdom pieces we
had written during the previous twenty-four hours at the festival.*

What does the first flame know? It knows how to grow!
What does the first flame learn? It learns how to burn!

We sang songs and we danced with all our youthful might.

Dance, maidens, dance, and we'll dance the song of freedom!
Maidens, dance, and we'll dance a song of peace.
Dance, dance, dance, let illusion slip away!
Maidens, dance and be free!

Twenty-one

IN MODERN AMERICAN SOCIETY, we traditionally "come of age" at
twenty-one. This is three-quarters of the way through the first Saturn
Cycle, the age of citizenship, and for many, graduation from college.
However, many young women take a different path.

Kristin observes:

*It seems strange to be a married woman and mother at
twenty-one, when most of my friends are single and almost all
are childless. I still think of myself in much the same way as I
did when I was seventeen, when I moved to this city and met my
husband. I certainly don't feel like a mother, although I look like
one.*

*Relatively early motherhood has gotten me somewhat out of
touch with what's typical for my age group—I've got responsibilities my friends can't imagine and don't want, but I've missed out
on the kind of experiences one associates with wild, careless
youth. I sometimes feel like I'm waiting for my life to start in that
respect, and the thought that it won't start until my son grows up
can sometimes get me down. There are so many things I'd like to
do, places I'd like to go, that simply aren't feasible with a family. I
have all the desires and impulses young women typically have at*

this time of life, to be spontaneous, promiscuous, reckless, but I have to practice a sometimes frustrating amount of restraint. It's often hard not to get bogged down in self-pity. I usually feel younger but act older than most twenty-one-year-olds, and that gets a little depressing.

A lot of things that were formerly illegal are now allowed. But as Ryan points out, "Yes, twenty-one defines you as an adult, but there aren't really a lot of perks involved. For example, the right to gamble, buy alcohol at a bar, and own a firearm . . . are all self-destructive things, so I don't think it's something to be so excited about."

From age twenty-one through twenty-three, Uranus squares itself, peaking in the twenty-second year, shaking up our sense of identity and forcing us to reconcile inner conflicts. When we resolve them, we will have a much better sense of who we are and what we want to be.

Turning twenty-one does not always bring the jubilant independence that young people expect. The nodes of the moon (the two endpoints of the moon's orbit through the sun's path) are returning to their natal position for the first time now. This carries with it a lot of soul searching and sometimes an overwhelming sense of loneliness. The self emerges from its chrysalis like a new butterfly, alone for the first time, and that wind can feel cold.

This new solitude is the key to adulthood. Keep calm, it will get easier in a while. But for the moment, this existential perception of the fact that we are now responsible for ourselves can create a lot of anxiety. You need to take some time off, to develop a social life, and explore your sexuality. A year or two spent working on social skills now will save you from becoming perpetually detached from life.

Sometimes we try to deal with it by a frantic search for connections and distraction—lovers, parties, drugs, alcohol. They numb the soul pain that can remain from traumatic memories, but they can also deaden perception. They can alter consciousness and lead to bonding, but if you indulge, before you make any commitments, find out how the person who seemed so attractive while you were stoned looks when you are straight. Be patient with yourself. Get out on your own and keep some time free to be alone and silent. Live long and prosper—death is forever, or at least for a good long time!

As Lynn says:

> *I love my life. I love being young in an age where women are no longer expected to be content with a life confined to their home, caring for the children. I can have whatever career I choose, whatever life I choose. Right now, I am pursuing a career as a writer, I am working on putting a band together, and I am working with a major recording group, booking gigs. I have managed to get the attention of one of my old crushes. He is just amazing. True, he lives in NYC, but things are working out. The last time he was in Boston, we spent time together. Despite all the current social unrest right now, I'd have to say that this is the best time to be young. I used to moan about having missed the 1960s. I can't complain anymore. I think this generation will be the one that will straighten it out—or get it started, anyway.*

THE BIRTHDAY

The twenty-first birthday is a milestone recognized by the larger society in which we live, though there is no real consensus on how it should be celebrated. Often, the celebration consists of getting the birthday girl drunk at the nearest bar. But in families where parents have shared a little dinner wine with their children from adolescence on, the first legal taste of alcohol is not much of a thrill.

The twenty-first birthday should be both a party and a ritual. This is the first day of the rest of your life as an adult. Invite your friends and older adults to whom you wish to demonstrate that you are worthy to join them. Plan a menu that reflects the way you hope you will be living.

At the beginning of the party, you might symbolize your past by wearing something characteristic of earlier years—perhaps something with a school logo, or simply a style that is no longer that of the person you want to be. Play music from the past few years. Decorate an ornamental arch in your favorite colors, or decorate the door that leads into your bedroom.

At an appropriate moment, call for silence. Stand in front of the gateway and make a short speech to thank those who have supported and inspired you, say what you value from your earlier years, and list the things from your past that you are now ready to leave behind. You may want to write these down on a piece of paper and then burn it in an ashtray.

Then you step through the door.

Go into another room in which you can change your clothes into something, preferably new, that suits the person that you want to become. Arrange with someone to put on new music, and announce you when you reappear. If you have friends who would enjoy helping, you may have escorts and attendants through this process.

Then step back through the gateway, a new adult and full member of the community. You may once more ask for silence and make a statement about your ideals and hopes for the future. At this point, friends and family may come forward to offer you advice, blessings, or gifts. Then, bring out the champagne! If the budget runs to a banquet, the blessings and statements may be covered through toasts and speeches after the dinner is done.

Twenty-two

AT TWENTY-TWO, THE ANXIETY BEGINS TO EASE UP. Well, a little. If we went to college straight out of high school we are graduating and looking for our first jobs. Now we step out onto the dance floor to get going on the real work of our First Destiny. The years between age twenty-two and twenty-nine are the most dynamic and formative period of our lives. We have the right to go where we please and do what we want, and we feel as if we will live forever.

It has taken us this long to get all the pieces together, body, mind, and spirit. During this year, your Saturn is squaring its natal position and so is Uranus. This is a gradual process, which may begin in your twenty-first year and complete itself when you are twenty-three. It tends to activate any unresolved internal conflicts. A facade of personal direction and courage may mask a deeper insecurity. We embark on the long road to responsibility, even though we may not truly achieve it until later. The foundations for all the cycles of maturation to follow are laid here.

Look around—what has excited you lately? A mission is hidden in that joy. At twenty-two, you need a mission, something to save, something to justify, something to rescue. It might be you, or you may decide it's time to save the world. It shouldn't be hard to find something that needs doing. Make your mistakes, but try to retain a sense of proportion. Get a mission, but don't get stuck in it—there will be many more. Environmental organizations can provide you with lists of ecological emergencies—find out what is going on. Something will "hum" at you and excite your passion, something that is worth losing sleep and comfort over, something that's worth risking jail.

If you have the courage, go up against entrenched authority. You have come into your power, and your work may change the world. Your concepts of social structure are taking shape, but by the time you reach age twenty-nine, they may change radically, so be careful—the more attached you become, the greater the change in that aspect of your life will be when Saturn returns.

Of course, there are some eras when changing the world seems more possible than others. Diana remembers her twenty-second year:

> I had moved to Berkeley to start graduate school the preceding autumn, just in time for the Free Speech Movement. The Civil Rights Movement had made unbelievable progress toward racial equality. It seemed clear that with a little more effort we might get this country to live up to its ideals in other areas as well. I found my niche editing a booklet on the Free Speech Movement for an Interfaith project. I did volunteer tutoring in the inner city, and debated whether I should become a missionary or join the Peace Corps.

THE BIRTHDAY

Throw a party and invite people who share your mission, or who have found inspiring missions of their own. In Northern Europe, it was an old folk custom to seal an oath by driving a nail into a doorframe or a tree. Get a length of 4" by 4" wood, a hammer, and some nails. As you describe your goal, hammer a nail into the board. Let your friends do the same. If the goal you've stated eventually turns out to be a dead end, you can pull out the nail later, but until then, the nails will bear witness to your determination to succeed.

Twenty-three

B Y THE AGE OF TWENTY-THREE our lives are really picking up speed. We are not only testing the waters, we are in the swim of things. If you haven't yet found your mission, look around you. What is the rest of your generation doing? Are they dancing? Are they making money? Are they trying out new careers? Are they starting families or still trying to break free?

There's a fine balance between caution and foolishness. Young lives can easily be lost if we don't pay attention, but we don't want to retreat from life either. The twenty-three-year-old who has no passion for anything is probably suffering from depression. Getting mentally healthy is a worthwhile mission too. Fortunately today there are many tools for healing minds. Take care of your head. If you can get through the next few years you will eventually outgrow the angst. Why not hang in there and see what's just around the corner?

At twenty-three, many of us are reworking our relationship with our parents. JoAnn reports that she spent most of this year in therapy, fighting depression and dealing with issues that had come up in relation to an abusive childhood.

Still others are cutting loose and taking off. Lucy says, "This was the year I finally fulfilled my longstanding dream of going to Europe. I went on a budget, staying at Youth Hostels and hitch-hiking. For three months I was on my own, with no family ties, no responsibilities, and only temporary human contacts. I discovered I could do just fine alone, but I don't think that's a very good way to live, so my goal now is to develop some relationships."

The sequence of events in one's twenties often depends on the age at which one leaves home. Those who began working right out of high school may have already made commitments and settled down. Z, who left home at sixteen, had two young children at this age. Men as well as women face these choices today. Michael says, "Being this age is great. Every year in my life is something new. New family members especially! I have two daughters and two nieces and one nephew. Being a young parent places a lot of responsibility on me. . . . I am an active kind of guy. A lot of people see it as a hassle to be the one person people depend on to move or help fix that fence, but not me. This is how I like to bond."

Parenthood is a developmental crisis for the parent as well as the child. Young parents need to watch their tempers, to recognize that their normal lives are going to be on hold until the children get older. The solution to parental stress is to put together a respite team. Partners should take turns watching the children. Involve the grandparents and train friends who aren't yet ready to become parents themselves to serve as part-time aunts and uncles.

THE BIRTHDAY

It's natural for our parents to want to celebrate our birthdays, and a family dinner is a fine thing to do. But at this age, your birthdays should be a triumph for you, not for your mother. Spend some time this birthday thinking about the kinds of ties—emotional, psychological, or economic—that still bind you to your parents. Write words representing those ties that need to be broken on a piece of white ribbon, tie it around your waist, and then cut it. After that, you can celebrate.

Twenty-four

FROM YEAR TWENTY-THREE ON, social horizons expand, and both friendship and mission are pursued with great energy. Jupiter's expansive energy is pushing you onward. The values you formed earlier are settled now, and it's a good thing, because you are likely to be too busy to do much philosophizing. Saturn is sextile to itself, a harmonious and supportive aspect that urges us to make commitments based on ethical considerations. Unlike the friends of our earlier years, who were likely to be chosen for us because they went to the same school or lived in the same neighborhood, the friendships of our twenties are based on affinity. Within the generational destiny we share, we can choose those whose missions match our own.

The first mission can manifest itself in unexpected ways. Diana recalls how she came to found the Society for Creative Anachronism:

> When I was twenty-three my social life focused on the Berkeley science fiction fan group. Two of the guys in the group had built medieval shields and swords and were trying to re-create European fighting techniques by experimentation. Since I often did fantasy illustrations for a fan magazine, I asked them to come demonstrate so I could make sketches.
>
> When they had gone home I got to thinking how much my friends who were studying medieval literature or reading Tolkien would enjoy seeing what sword fighting really looked like. Then, like the proverbial lightbulb going off, it came to me—we could hold a tournament in our backyard! The idea, of course, was ridiculous. I was supposed to be getting ready for my Master's exams. I went inside and said to my roommates, "I just had this wacky idea, please talk me out of it!" They all responded, "That sounds neat—let's do it!"
>
> Thus, the Society for Creative Anachronism was born. I made fliers that ended up all over the Bay Area. Fifty people came; we had sword fighting and dancing, poetry and feasting, and a march down Telegraph Avenue to protest the twentieth century.

It was a great success. By the end of the day people were talking about doing it again.

By the time I was twenty-four we had a magazine, a regular schedule of events, and were busy researching medieval music, dancing, and costume as well as fighting. My training in medieval research had turned out to be useful after all. For the next ten years I was one of the group's leaders. The Society gave me a husband and some wonderful friends, changed my life and that of a good many other people, and is still, as of this writing, going strong. . . .

THE BIRTHDAY

This year, celebrate your friendships. Ask two or three of the people closest to you to join you in something you will all really enjoy. Go to a concert or take a camping trip.

Twenty-five

TOWARD THE END OF THE TWENTY-FOURTH YEAR and into the twenty-fifth Saturn has been moving through a harmonious relationship to the position it held in your birth chart. This will push you toward deep commitment to people or causes. Your mission will call forth all of your loyalty and devotion, shaped by an increased ethical sensitivity. At twenty-five, your mission peaks.

The first steps in your chosen profession also start you on your mission. For others, the job is a way to support yourself while you "follow your bliss." You need to take care of yourself, make sure you eat and sleep enough to maintain the energy levels you'll need. For some, like those musicians who began studying in childhood, the mid-twenties are a time of mastery of the instrument and the beginning of success in their profession. But sometimes the mission is not what we thought it was going to be. In her mid-twenties Nadia Boulanger realized that her real gift lay not in composing, but in teaching.

Whatever your goal, take a deep breath and go for it. These years can see stunning success or a trail of missed opportunities. Say "Yes" to everything except what might kill you!

Amy writes:

> *I think turning twenty-five was something of a milestone for me. I'm really starting to feel like an "adult" lately. I moved into my first "real" apartment (before this I was in studios that felt like dorm rooms). I am more mature and centered in who I am and what I want out of life. I have wonderful, stable relationships with two men who care deeply for me. I find my mind turning to motherhood a bit more. I used to say I'd never have a child. Then a dear friend had a baby. Helping with her little one has tripped something in me (as I knew it might) and my thoughts have turned to the possibility, but it's still down the road for me.*

THE BIRTHDAY

Celebrate your own "Silver Anniversary" by honoring Artemis, goddess of the silver moon and patroness of young women. Spend an afternoon hiking or in some other sport. If weather permits and the moon is in a visible phase, set up a Moon-Watching Party. Wear white and silver. Have a white cake; drink champagne from a silver goblet; give all your guests new quarter coins as keepsakes.

Twenty-six

YOU'RE TWENTY-SIX YEARS OLD, and you're wondering just what you've accomplished and where to go from here! Don't worry— you may not see the fruits of your First Destiny until much later. It was only at this age, for instance, that Jane Goodall finally was able to begin the field study of chimpanzees that has become her life work. If you have not yet found a way to address your deepest needs and desires, get busy, because the pressure will become painful if you don't do something about it now. You are approaching the end of your First Destiny, but you still have time and energy to develop your current interests. In two more years you will be swinging into your first Saturn Return, and then your priorities are likely to change.

Play more, be more creative. Don't be afraid of ambition—make a big move, try something new. At this age, we feel invincible. But remember that this destiny is only your first. Once you are past it, your feelings will change. So don't jump into something just because you are "almost thirty," but because it is calling to you.

The lesson for this year is to try new things, but don't get stuck. The one exception is love—if you have already found the love of your life, congratulations. But remember that love, too, is cyclical. This may not be the year to find the love that ends all loves.

THE BIRTHDAY

Twenty-six is an inventory year, a time to examine your soul, see where it hurts, and do something about it. Get this process started on your birthday. Whatever other celebrations are planned, take some time to go off by yourself with a notebook. In one column list your dreams. What are your secret ambitions? If your life ended tomorrow, what would you wish you had done? In the other column, list one step you can take in that direction. That's how every journey begins—with a single step.

Twenty-seven

AFTER LAST YEAR'S RENEWAL we are busy once more. We may not even notice our birthday. We have hit our strides, and the projects created by our mission are all around us. New doors are opening, and we are eager to step through them. But we need to be careful not to take on so much that there's no time to have a life as well.

In the midst of all this activity you may notice an occasional sense of dissatisfaction, a malaise that you don't quite understand. This is because the work of your First Destiny is moving toward a conclusion.

It may not be obvious, but something within you senses it. The shift will be gradual, so for the time being, keep on with your work, fulfill your responsibilities, and enjoy your social contacts. This destiny is almost over—make the most of it.

As Jesa says:

> *Twenty-seven feels like twenty-six, only a bit more hectic and crazed. The decisions I made when I didn't have enough wisdom to make them are coming back full circle and often slapping me in the face. I'm forced to re-examine my personality, my motives, and my dreams. I feel increasing pressure to figure out what I want in life, to realize my calling and take steps toward it. I focus inward more and outward more too. I am finding my voice and noticing that I have something to say and to contribute to the world. Sometimes it hurts—a lot—but these are growing pains and I welcome them more every day. It is tangible proof that I am growing, maturing. I am learning to love myself.*

Melanie also feels the pressure as her first Saturn Return approaches:

> *I am introspective anyway, but this year has been even more so. For lack of a better, less crude phrase, I've been trying to "get my s**t together." The need to decide what I want to be when I grow up has hit a critical level. . . . My problem is that I feel drawn to so many things, so this has been a year of discovering new talents, abilities, and interests.*
>
> *Tied in with the career angst is the need for synthesis. I feel that I have different "parts" of myself that are at times warring with one another. Dwelling within me is an earth mama who wants to be all-natural, not wear makeup, live in flowing skirts and bare feet, eat organic foods, and be at peace with the earth and all her creatures. But there is also the hip urban city girl who loves all the trappings of being situated near a metropolis, finds rush hour traffic exhilarating, wants to dye her hair funky colors and wear cool shoes and hang out in artsy bookstores and coffee houses.*

I wage inner battles between believing that fat is a feminist issue, embracing my Willendorf-esque figure and feeling that the best way to honor the Goddess inherent in myself is to treat my body healthily and lose weight. One day I want children desperately, the next day the mere thought of giving up that much of my life is horrifying. On the good side, I have come into my voice and learned to stand up for myself and to speak my truth. I take better care of myself and realize that I have much inside me that is valuable. . . . Part of this is a reawakening to the spiritual. Having rejected the Christianity of my childhood back in college, I was floating along believing that I was just fine without a spiritual connection. But the call of the Goddess became too strong, and as I work with her and honor her presence in my life I find some of these questions beginning to work their way toward answers. . . . Perhaps the best thing that twenty-seven has taught me is that the journey itself is the destination.

New desires will grow in you as your restlessness increases. You may find release in your sexuality, which at this age is ripe and demanding. Share your love with a partner—or play the field. Serendipity is looking for you, so allow for unplanned events to occur. Go places on the spur of the moment. Learn something new.

THE BIRTHDAY

Have a Serendipity Birthday! Don't make plans for this one, beyond alerting a friend or two. On the morning of your birthday, get a newspaper and flip through it, looking for something that takes your fancy to do. Go window shopping—your friends can buy presents for you as you go. Stop somewhere that looks good for a meal. Who knows where you might end up?

Twenty-Eight

HERE COMES THE HINGE! Between destinies, life gives us a space like the hinge on a door. The hinge itself moves very little, but it swings the door wide. Such is our position at this time in our lives. Life may seem to have come to a standstill, but it isn't so. We're entering that time of transition, a cosmic turning point from one destiny to the next, and the careful hands of the fates are guiding us through.

Maeve's advice is, "Take what you can get and make it better, steal what you need in order to survive, live through the grace and benevolence of others, also keep your personal debts free and clear, live for today, don't be afraid of tomorrow, and short of death nothing in life is so terrible that you have to beat yourself up over it."

Although this is the year that Saturn returns to its natal position in your chart, the transition period may extend through the next three or four years. Exactly how this goes will depend on who you are and what your First Destiny has been like, but a normal hinge period can come anywhere from age twenty-eight to thirty-two, depending on the other aspects around Saturn and your own readiness.

It is a dangerous time. Those who are careless may die. Attempts at suicide are more likely to succeed. Some people only get one destiny. Don't get hysterical with the idea that your world is collapsing. It is supposed to. The seeds of a new cycle have been planted, but you have to give them time. For the present, you will just have to live with ambiguity.

Lisa has a lot to say about being on the hinge:

> *Although I am still considered very young or naive in many circles, I have days where I feel as though I am very wise and literally the oldest in the room. I've learned that love is a compromise, one you make with yourself and not with others—where you give a piece of your heart away, even if you don't always receive one in return.*
>
> *I've learned that marriage is hard work and that divorce is easy.*

I've learned that nothing in life is free and that I've earned everything I have—the smiles from my friends, tears from my child, my relationship with the Goddess. They've all cost me something and the memories are priceless.

I've found friends who are committed, and those that need to be—but they're mine, and I love them. They believe in me.

I've learned that there is no such thing as a "do-over."

I've learned that my parents really were right and that school can be fun, that moms really aren't perfect, and that money doesn't grow on trees.

I've learned that I am a WOMAN, not a girl, chick, or babe—but occasionally I am a "Honey."...

I've learned that there is so much more to discover and that I've only just begun, and that I look forward to the ride no matter how bumpy it gets.

THE BIRTHDAY

Saturn, the old man of the skies, is rolling into your life, so get him in a good mood with a party for him and his wife, the goddess Ops (from whose name comes our word *opulence*). In Roman mythology, Saturnus and Ops ruled during the Golden Age when everyone was equal and all prospered. So have as rich and opulent a party as you can provide. If it's a potluck, all your guests will share in the good magic. Have good wine, rich desserts, chocolate.... Set a plate of food and drink in front of a picture of Saturn and welcome his energy!

Twenty-nine

IF LAST YEAR FELT AS IF EVERYTHING HAD STOPPED, by the time you reach the age of twenty-nine, you know you're moving. If you think it's going to get easier, think again—the hinge is still turning.

This shifting within you—did you catch it? Attitudes are changing, values are transforming. Suddenly, things you thought you could not live without must be discarded or . . . die. . . . Suicidal thoughts can threaten to overwhelm you. You have to ignore them.

At the end of the twenties you may feel, "I am almost thirty and I am still not a millionaire, married, a parent. . . ." You fill in the blank. But there is no law that says you have to do anything before you are thirty but complete your twenty-ninth year! Balance on this bridge between destinies. Pull yourself together and endure the transition with grace and safety.

As those things in your life that are really unnecessary are torn away, your new family/friends/occupation/mission are slowly emerging, so try to enjoy the sea change. Allow the timeless sense of the hinge space to calm your anxieties. Enjoy those passions that remain from your First Destiny even as you watch for the first tender shoots of new life to emerge.

Some people get married (or remarried) at this time. Kate remembers the day she met her husband:

> He and a friend came by to collect money for the mass exodus of friends to see the re-release of Return of the Jedi. . . . I got up long enough to say hello and hand over my check. Just behind my friend was this guy in a leather trench coat and fedora. I looked at him, he looked at me, and I felt something . . . a jolt, and click . . . a knowing. I remember filing the knowing-ness away for later thought and going back to writing. . . . I "knew" he would be at the Ostara ritual and there he was. He found the Goddess Egg and gave it to me, just as I knew he would, and later that night, talking till some ungodly hour, we realized that we had invoked each other into our lives. I never used to believe in love at first sight, but . . . something sure happened to us!

Women and men often have similar attitudes when it comes to making a commitment. Brad, who got married at this age, recalls the pre-marriage counseling at his father's church:

> One of the questions was, "If everything in your marriage goes completely wrong, what is the one thing you can rely on that

the two of you will still have?" The first and second couples
looked at each other all starry-eyed and said, "Love." When the
pastor got to us, I was first. I looked him straight in the eye and
said, "Communication!"... My bride-to-be answered the same....
The first two couples blurted out, "Oh yeah, we have that, too!"...
Later, after the session, the pastor complimented us on our
answer and our conviction.

But making such a commitment before you have finished your transformation may be risky—when you're done you may not be the same person. It's best to wait until you are settled into your Second Destiny to marry. Then you'll have a better chance for a partnership that will last a long time.

Remember, whatever you do now will begin to shape your next twenty-eight years....

Chrys reflects on being twenty-nine and a member of "Gen X":

I am twenty nine and a mother of two beautiful kids....
How do I feel in my skin? Pretty damn good. I am proud to be part
of Gen X (which for many years I hated being called), but now
that I'm closer to my thirties I feel it's okay to be labeled that.
It's a bit frustrating though sometimes to be part of my genera-
tion. We are always stereotyped as "slackers," "lame," and my
personal fave, "uneducated." (Oops, I forgot the all-time low,
"disrespectful"!)

Growing up in the 1980s was sometimes fun, and always a
challenge. Street drugs, teen pregnancy, AIDS, eating disorders,
domestic violence, divorce, and homelessness all made the head-
lines, but became issues that nobody wanted to really deal with
or talk about honestly. I sometimes looked around my middle-
class suburban nightmare and wondered what the hell were all
these adults thinking/doing?...

All of Reagan's good old boys messed our economy up so bad
that most of my generation cannot afford to buy their own
houses, cars, etc., the way that all of my mother's and father's
generation did, as well as my grandparents before them. Does

that make sense? We have to struggle much harder than those who came before us, and it leaves me feeling bitter.

There's so much hard work to do, and so much negativity to unravel—I know that we can do it, though.

Growing up in the '80s also meant latchkey kids, guns at school, a substandard school system (in most cases), and many kids falling through the cracks one way or another (like myself), and having messed-up parents and no one to turn to (which a huge percent of us have had to live through—yes, Courtney Love knew what she was talking about).

But all in all, I'm still proud to be a part of an intelligent, balls/ovaries to the wall group of kids who have taken major strides to end racism and sexism, and have the courage to protest against the evil that our government tries to spoon-feed us on a daily basis (yes, I still hate Tipper Gore).

I sometimes wish that the baby-boomers would cut us some slack and open their eyes to us and respect what we have accomplished in the world. . . .

THE BIRTHDAY

To counteract the "I'm almost thirty and I haven't . . ." syndrome, use this birthday to celebrate the things you *have* done. Celebrate the deeds of your First Destiny. Tape a big piece of butcher paper on the wall. List each year since age twenty and next to it write down what you were doing. Have pencils available—friends who come to your party may add more and surprise you.

Thirty

THIRTY IS A WATERSHED YEAR. Saturn's slow grind is carrying us onward. Whatever our plans were, they are only chapters in a big book that he is writing. At thirty, we know something is going on.

Think of yourself as a patient on the operating table. You can't get up and run away because the universe is working on you. You need to stay closed down, be patient while Saturn rearranges your body, mind, and soul. By the time this year is over you will be getting down to the basics that will carry you through the next thirty years.

Keep your eyes open—your next mission should be coming into view any time now. Meanwhile, pick and choose those things from your past that you want to take with you, enjoy life, and don't worry about getting old!

THE BIRTHDAY

Who do you trust? Who trusts you? Make a list of those things and people you can really depend on. In some cases you may be wrong, for they are changing too, but the effort will give you some stability. Have a party to celebrate getting through your twenties. Invite all your favorite people and thank them for helping you get this far.

Burn one brown candle (for the fertile earth) for where you've been and two green ones (for growth) to help you move on. You can light them in private or put them in the middle of your birthday cake, or you can take them to burn in a cemetery. The thirtieth birthday is a good time to visit the ancestors—birthdays and deathdays are the two sides of the same door. If you can't visit the place where your own family is buried, take a walk through the nearest cemetery and find a spot that seems friendly. Adopt an untended grave and take care of it. Light your candles and some incense and make a prayer like this one:

> *Ancestors! You whose DNA is in my body,*
> *you who still live through me,*
> *protect me from foolishness and fear,*
> *send me health, wealth, and wisdom,*
> *the holy three!*
> *As I wish, so mote it be!*

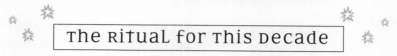

The Ritual for This Decade

WALKING THE LABYRINTH: A RITE OF PASSAGE THROUGH THE HINGE

A ritual to celebrate the first Saturn Return can be performed at any time during the three or four years in which the shift is going on. However, we recommend waiting until the changes are apparent and you feel a real need to understand them.

The purpose of the ritual is to take you through an experience that reflects what is happening to you on the psychological and spiritual level, so that you can integrate your conscious understanding with your intuitive awareness. It also helps friends and family to recognize that the person you are becoming is not quite the same as the one they have known.

The symbol for this turning in your life is the labyrinth, that ancient pattern that leads inward to the center and then out again. It has appeared everywhere from ancient Cretan carvings to Native American baskets. When you walk the labyrinth, the twists and turnings by which you return to the outside world are not quite the same as those by which you entered.

For this rite, therefore, you will need to construct a labyrinth. The most common pattern is the one illustrated here.

THE LABYRINTH

A labyrinth may be constructed by setting out stones, drawing the pattern on a smooth floor, outlining it in duct tape, or inscribing it on the beach on the smooth sand. Some have made a permanent and portable labyrinth by painting the pattern on one or several plastic or canvas painters' dropcloths taped together. A book that offers excellent directions for constructing a labyrinth, as well as inspiring ideas for using them, is *Labyrinth,* by Melissa Gayle West (for full information, see the Resources at the end of this book). One of our favorite permanent labyrinths is on the grounds of Grace Cathedral in San Francisco.

The ritual itself should be followed by a party. Designate a friend to take charge of the food and service at the event.

The spiritual powers honored in this rite are the Three Sisters known variously as the Fates or the Norns, who Z describes in her book *Summoning the Fates.* With the first Saturn Return, you pass from the power of Urdh, who rules the past, into that of Verdandi, who governs that which is becoming. Of course, any time you make a change in your life you are working with these two fate goddesses, but in this ritual you will feel the dynamic tension between them in a more powerful way.

Since you are working with the powers of Saturn, the obvious day on which to hold your ritual is a Saturday. Invite friends who you want to witness your transition. Gifts are appropriate, but not necessary. At the center of the labyrinth, place a stool or cushion to sit on, and a chalice or bowl full of spring water. Wear new clothes, but over them put on an old caftan, loose robe, or drapery (even an old curtain or bedspread will do).

Ask a friend to get everyone standing in a circle around the labyrinth. Let her read the instructions for the ritual ahead of time, and get someone to agree to lead the song. To the regular beat of a drum, enter the room and pause before the entry to the labyrinth. Turn to the others and explain that you have come here to change your fate by seeking the Well of Wisdom. You are willing to give up whatever is unnecessary or outworn in order to find your destiny.

Then enter the labyrinth. As you do so, everyone begins to sing:

It's time for turning,

It's time to seek the source within;

It's time for learning

To bring that wisdom back again. . . .

Walk slowly. Each time you come to a turning, remember some significant moment or relationship in your life that is over, or something that you want to give up, and consciously leave it behind. As you move toward the center of the labyrinth, imagine you are moving into the center of the Earth, where the Norns wait by the Well beneath the roots of the Worldtree.

When you get to the center, sit down. At this point the others should change from singing to a soft, wordless humming. Close your eyes and relax.

See in your mind's eye the image of the Well of Wyrd, from which all fate flows. Imagine that you can see a veiled woman sitting beside it. This is Verdandi, the Norn who rules that which is coming into existence. Think about what you hope your new destiny will bring, and then look into the well. Ask for a vision of your new destiny.

When you feel that the experience is complete, open your eyes, take up the chalice of spring water, and drink.

When you have finished the water, pull off the garment or drapery that covered your new clothes, and let it fall to the ground. At this point everyone can sing the chant once more. Make your way through the return path of the labyrinth. Take it slowly, allowing new impressions to form, noting your feelings and sensations. When you reach the exit, stop as everyone applauds. If you feel able, share what you have learned with your friends. Move around the circle to be hugged, first by the leader and then by all your friends. Then continue on to food, presents, and celebration.

AGES 31 TO 40

Carousel

B Y THE TIME WE BEGIN OUR THIRD DECADE we have a good seat on the Carousel of Life and are reaching for the brass ring! We are launched upon the Second Destiny. These are the years when we will flower and bear fruit. We not only know enough to be effective, but we have the energy to carry out our ideas. Our generation is coming into its own.

Congratulations on having made it to the age of thirty! Not everyone gets that far. But although you may have taken a few knocks, you have survived your First Destiny, and we welcome you. Step right up, get on that horse—and wait.... Because, my friend, you may have stepped into your Second Destiny, but the Carousel is still warming up. Take a deep breath and wait for the stars.

At the beginning of your thirties, Saturn, who moved into your life sometime after your twenty-eighth birthday, is still lumbering through. He comes in and gives you a push, then spends a couple of years while you discuss things. You get ready for a big change, and then for a while it may seem that nothing is happening, but the seeds are being planted, hidden within. Florence Nightingale, who had dreamed of becoming a nurse for years, was not able to actually start training until she was thirty-one. Three years later, she was running the British Army's Nursing Service in the Crimean War, a mission that made her a national hero and allowed her to change the role and status of nurses forever. In her early thirties, Betty Friedan had the insights and began the work that resulted in *The Feminine Mystique*.

These are the proverbial "I want to find myself" years. The urge to move, to change, is incredibly strong—pain may come with it, just to kick you into full adulthood. There is nothing as potent as sheer misery to change one's attitude. This is a time for deep remorse and soul searching. Being on the hinge can really hurt.

To survive, learn how to stand up to it. Don't run and hide—kick back somewhere all by yourself and meditate. Allow your deep mind to come out and play—doing nothing may be the most important thing you can do right now. It will speed up the moment when you "sight" your new goal. Have faith; in time, you will see a clear picture and know how to act on it. Spirituality will be coupled with action.

People have their own ways of dealing with the hinge. Even when things look darkest, when all you can see is what you are losing, don't despair. There is a whole lot more hidden on the other side of that door. Life gives us information on a "need to know" basis, turning one page at a time. At thirty, you can't say where you'll be in ten years, but the blueprint is in your DNA, and in the stars.

After about three years of turmoil, Saturn has done his job, packs his bags, and moves on, leaving you with the revelation of your new mission in life.

Diana reflects on how much easier it is to identify the significant events of the hinge years with hindsight:

> *The year I turned twenty-eight, although I didn't realize it at the time, everything in my life began to change. At the beginning of the year, I realized that I had time on my hands at my secretarial job, and started writing a novel. As a teenager I had dreamed*

of being a writer, but in college decided it wasn't "practical." But I'd also had the ambition to produce either a child or a book before I was thirty. I had the child, but it was clear to me that although I could help him grow, he was his own creative project, not mine. A novel, I thought, would be my own.

In the three years that followed, the focus of my creativity shifted from the Society for Creative Anachronism to the fictional world I was creating. I realized that it was unfair to expect people to be my creative medium. The organization was growing, and it was becoming clear that it was time to allow new leadership to take over.

By the time I was through the hinge, I had found my Second Destiny.

We are always living through two destinies—our personal story, and the species destiny. Newspaper astrology columns give us the personal perspective, based on sun signs, but this individual destiny is played out in the context of the fates of the other members of our species with whom we are traveling through this life. Everyone in our generation has a different story, but the turning points in our lives are the same, determined by the stars. Whether or not we are aware of it, we have parts in a celestial drama, a cosmic soap opera that's still going on. At the end of the first Saturn Return, we have an opportunity to pick and choose those elements from our pasts that we want to carry into our new lives, and leave the rest behind.

Earth herself is another player. Drought and flood, hurricane and earthquake return to shake the Earth in their seasons. We have the illusion of independence, but we are a minor part of the entity that we call Gaia, living on 5 percent of her topsoil. And the Earth is only one planet in a solar system that is part of the universe where the celestial sisters continue their eternal dance. One of the great illuminations of the '60s came from those photos of the fragile blue planet that is our home.

We also exist in a cultural environment. We create commerce and culture, the products that benefit or harm us. Birds sing, but we make music that expresses the spirit of each age. Animals eat, but we create cuisine. What we have to remember is that when others are starving, our spirits are malnourished, even if our bodies have food.

All these things are the warp on the loom of life, through which we weave our own destinies. You begin your Second Destiny as a full adult, and it will shape your life until the end of your fifties. There will be many twists and turnings, but hang on. This is your prime time, the reward for making it through your First Destiny. Make the most of it!

FATE DATES FOR AGES 31 TO 40			
Ages 32–33	♆ ✳ ♆	Neptune sextiles self	•Deepening understanding of purpose for generation
	♀ ✳ ♀	Pluto sextiles self	•A tricky, transitional age
Age 36	♃ ☌ ♃	Jupiter returns	•Finding a niche and life work •Possible promotion, expanding horizons
Ages 37–42	♅ ☍ ♅	Uranus opposes self	•Need for independence •Crisis can signal a change in purpose, lifestyle, goals, and direction •Possible inner conflict can lead to new identity •Stress and danger
	♆ □ ♆	Neptune squares self	•Loss of old ideals, develop new ones
	☊☋	Moon nodes return	•Reappraise goals and relationships
Ages 37–44	♄ □ ♄	Saturn squares self	•Change is imperative

Thirty-one

B Y THE BEGINNING OF OUR THIRTIES, most of us have left our parents' homes (although sometimes we've been forced by circumstances to temporarily move back again!). But throughout the twenties we may have still depended on our parents for some financial as well as emotional support. Or you may have taken refuge in an early marriage or relationship. Only when you become independent will your Second Destiny unfold. Whenever it occurs, this separation is like birth—you emerge as a newborn adult, ready to set forth on the path you will follow for the next thirty years.

This separation is usually traumatic. At this point, your emotional life may change. Some women discover that they are gay or bisexual, find a new mate, or decide to go it alone. Adric reports that gay men, who usually "come out" during their twenties, in their thirties discover that the first flush of youth is gone, and they may need to explore different aspects of the gay lifestyle.

You may choose a new family and friends, set new goals.

Lannette reports, "At age thirty-one, after much inner work ... I've finally realized that I truly don't need a man in my life to feel complete. I spent my entire adult life wanting someone to rescue me, and I just ended up resenting those men who tried. My independence and my self-reliance are now two of my most treasured traits."

Be careful, these choices can make or break you. But don't let the uncertainty that Saturn brings make you freeze like a deer in the headlights. Some people respond to the challenge by refusing it. If you stop developing at this stage you will never mature.

Z remembers:

> *At thirty, I tried both refusing and accepting the challenge of*
> *full adulthood. My first reaction was to freeze in the karmic*
> *winds. I attempted suicide, which, thank the Goddess, comically*
> *failed. Then, still almost unable to eat or talk, I left home and*
> *family behind in New York and hitchhiked to California.*

By the time I was thirty-one, I had an apartment in Santa Monica and was living alone for the first time. For over ten years I had cleaned up after husband and children, and now it was only me. In delight I followed the traces of this new woman. Who was she?

I loved her—she did thoughtful things, watered plants, cleaned the apartment. She was not lonely because she had just given birth to herself, which is what the Women's Liberation Movement was all about. My generation was waking up to liberation. We gathered together and shared our experience as women, listening to each other. For the first time, many of us realized we shared a pain that came from being women in a society that didn't like women! It is hard to swallow this concept when you are a heterosexual mother of sons.

I was nurtured and supported by the friendship of the other women with whom I shared this historical awakening. It was sublime. I was happy at last. I volunteered to staff the Women's Center on Mondays. I read all the pamphlets and books about women. I made my womanhood a study and an art.

Before my thirty-first year was out I had started the very first Feminist Witches' group—the Susan B. Anthony Coven #1. Womanhood dominated my imagination and my spirituality. By the end of the next year, women were coming from all over. I was a fledgling High Priestess with an ad hoc coven, and I had found my Second Destiny.

THE BIRTHDAY

You're on the Carousel, so you might as well have fun with it! Make the Merry-Go-Round the theme for your birthday party. Have a picnic at the park and ride the carousel. As you go round and round, relax into the motion, shout and sing!

Thirty-two

B Y THIS TIME, MOST OF THE DUST has settled from the upsets of your Saturn Return. You may find yourself with a brand-new life— a new home, a new job, your own taxes, or a new family. A woman who bears children in her thirties probably already has a career, and will face difficult choices when it comes to child care.

Hired baby-sitters should be the last choice for regular help. No employee will love your child as keenly as someone who has a personal relationship with her. Explore the possibility of sharing child care with a relative or close friend. Choose a reputable agency when hiring paid help, and make sure the sitter understands principles of safety and where the limits for discipline are. Avoid hiring teenagers to look after infants. Their short attention span makes them undependable with babies. Older women, even seniors who are fit and alert, are a better choice. They have a steady, calm vibration that will soothe and relax the child.

Parenthood is never easy, but it helps if you make an alliance with the spirit world. Daily prayer with the child is a good practice that helps the child become aware of the spirit within and acknowledges and nourishes it. Childhood spirituality provides a foundation on which other spiritual practices can be built.

Z still remembers a goodnight prayer her aunt taught her many years ago. Its very simplicity affirms her ancestral connections:

> *"My God, good God, I close my eyes tonight, but yours stay open. While I sleep you watch over me. Bless my parents and my little brother so that when morning arrives we can kiss each other again. Blessed be."*
>
> *My "little brother" is now forty-seven, but I am sure this prayer helped him get there. And my parents, bless them, are twenty-five years gone.*

Most cultures have some concept of a guardian spirit, whether it be an angel or an ancestor. An ancestor, especially if your own mother or grandmother is not available to advise you, can filter wise counsel on child rearing into your head if you open yourself up to hear.

Pay attention to the collective visions of your generation. As you move into your thirties, Neptune the Dream-Maker is sextile to his natal position, a particularly harmonious aspect. He may bring you some lucky insights and stimulate your imagination. Pluto, the Generation-Definer, is also sextile, and his influence will increase. Watch for truths that you have overlooked to rise up from the depths.

Now is the time to learn what your generation is all about. What is your age group's collective purpose? Pluto and Neptune move slowly, bringing in historic changes that serve as a backdrop for your personal evolution.

THE BIRTHDAY

By now, many of your friends are probably through their Saturn Return as well. Invite them for a birthday dinner. The first toast will be for you, but you should propose the second. Ask each guest to salute the most important thing that she or he has learned during the past five years. Try to move the conversation into a discussion of where your generation is going.

Thirty-three

OH, HOW CHILDHOOD HAUNTS US! Neptune and Pluto are both sextile to themselves, forcing us to consider our relationship to our generation. Thirty-three is a time for immature emotions to grow up. But for that to happen, we need nurturing, just as we did when we were children. Now, however, we nurture ourselves. If your childhood was unhappy, create a different scenario for yourself. Take advantage of self-help books and groups. Remember the definition of the role of the Mother given in the Womanhood ritual in the chapter on ages 11 to 20. When we move into the life stage of the Mother, we become our own mothers. We must raise our new selves to become the people we want to be.

Ellen reports that she spent the better part of age thirty-three working with the Strength card from the tarot. "I did a lot of growth around being Strength and being Strong. I found that this has grounded me more fully in myself, my truth, and my honesty. I am no less nice, yet I am clearer about my boundaries and the rules for playing in my sandbox (as it were)."

Regina comments:

> *I love my age, myself, my body, and my life. I was a late bloomer but have grown to know and accept that I cannot do all things, be everyone's friend, always please my parents, and that I am not super mom. I have also come to realize and accept that I am comfortable with being bisexual, that I am a big, beautiful woman, I will never let a man hit me again, my self-esteem is mine, and I control it. I am a goddess and she is in me, but most of all I am proud to be a healer as a licensed nurse and as a natural world healer, a witch.*

This age is a delicate time, when adult ego development occurs. We have endured the shock of Saturn's return and now we will ease into social interaction with our newborn selves. We are still tender, but our new selves are clearly defined. Now comes the challenge. We have to get out into the wider world and make something of ourselves, use our talents, find where to make our contribution. We want to be seen as individuals, not as the children of our parents. We are obeying an instinctive urge.

The work of the Second Destiny is well begun.

THE BIRTHDAY

In J. R. R. Tolkien's *Lord of the Rings,* we learn that hobbits don't come of age until they are thirty-three. Take this opportunity to celebrate your own emergence into your Second Destiny with a hobbit birthday party. This means *lots* of food and drink, singing and dancing. For the contents of a hobbit's pantry, on which to base a menu, re-read the opening chapter of *The Hobbit.*

Thirty-four

THIS IS A YEAR FOR CLEAR-COASTING. We are still delicate, but things are moving. At this age we need inner stillness, like a fisherwoman on a clear blue sea, alert, but also still.

The fertility cycle is at its height. For some, the "motherhood" chimes are ringing, and our drive toward social interaction pushes us to make a family. It's a good time to make babies—nothing speeds up maturation like becoming a parent yourself.

But there are other kinds of fertility. Especially if you have already borne your children, you may be eager for more training in a new field, or new relationships may open up other possibilities.

Z remembers:

> At this age I was in love with a woman. She was a little younger, from the Midwest. I loved my shy, brainy, beautiful lover. Where men had given me grief, she supported my dream of women's spirituality. I finally moved in with her in Santa Monica. She was a Libra, I, an Aquarian. She was teaching people how to maintain and repair Volkswagen bugs, which is what most of us had for cars. I made my living by gardening and cleaning houses. On sabbats I was a High Priestess who could call for natural miracles. At night she was my safe harbor. I wrote articles and published with other women a newspaper called Sisters. We were working the L.A. area feminist circles. We had Food Conspiracies, shopping in the early morning for cheap food. We started a rape hotline, opened a second Women's Center in Santa Monica. These were rich, productive times.

THE BIRTHDAY

Make your new interests the focus for your birthday party. Invite people you are working with to meet your other friends and family. Give each person a chance to talk about what she or he is doing and why it's important. You may be surprised by what you hear. Too often, we keep our friends in separate mental "boxes," which means we miss all of the richness that can come from interaction.

Thirty-five

THIS YEAR MAY FEEL VERY DIFFERENT from the last. This is the last call for your Second Destiny to reveal itself. If you haven't already found a new direction, you will this year. For many, the new destiny is already filling your consciousness, and it feels good. That's important—life should not be a valley of tears. Most of the things we are supposed to be doing feel great, so if your fated path is the right one, it will give you satisfaction and excitement. It's a win/win situation!

Isina reports, "At thirty-five, I have more confidence in myself and my abilities than ever before. I am starting to love myself for who I am rather than hate myself for who I'm not."

Still, life may give you a jolt to make sure you are listening. When Z was thirty-five, she was arrested for tarot reading. "The nerve-wracking thing was being tried as a witch. You go to court, sit there with your back to the audience, and listen to a lawyer talk about your religion as inherently fraudulent. I lost the trial but won public opinion, appealed, and won legally nine years later."

Diana's thirty-fifth year was eventful as well:

> *After seven years of sending out manuscripts and getting them back again, my first two short stories were published. But Saturn had a last gift for me—a friend asked me to put together a coming-of-age ritual for her, which resulted in the founding of Darkmoon Circle, a women's spirituality group which is still going over twenty years later, and was the real beginning of my work as a priestess.*

So this age can be eventful while still developing in the direction Saturn's return has started you. After this year you are on the way.

THE BIRTHDAY

If this year is going to be eventful, you need to get ready! Invite people who give you real support to your party. Give them gifts and let them know how much you appreciate their love and friendship.

Thirty-six

A GREAT YEAR! Jupiter is making his regular twelfth year visit back to his natal position, bringing visibility, wealth, health, friends, and noble purpose. This was certainly true for Marie Curie, whose pioneering work on radium won her a Nobel Prize and world fame. Good luck returns to our lives. This influence will help you to find your niche. It generates a huge burst of energy. This is prime time, when we have a maximum of energy for everything—sex, food and drink, work, love—we can't get enough of them. This is a time for our great work. Our intellect expands, and with it our vision. Jupiter's return often brings a promotion, or puts us in a position with broader horizons. Fate takes a deep breath and then moves us toward the fulfillment of our dreams.

Diana of Seven Pines says, "I am thirty-six, and my age is 'sturdy.' I am settled, my roots have dug deep, and I can withstand the forces that push at me and try to change my direction and focus."

THE BIRTHDAY

Make this birthday party an opportunity to celebrate Jupiter's coming blessings. Have a toga party. Decorate with royal blue, Jupiter's color. Serve rich and yummy food, and lots to drink. Dance!

Thirty-seven

FOR SOME, THIRTY-SEVEN CAN BE A PUZZLE. Some think of it as a "non-number" symbolically, but there's a lot going on in the stars. Saturn has moved out of his natal position and is now squaring it. This is the same astrological configuration as in your seventh year. You are now in a position of strength. Buy that house, settle down to that big project. You can also allow unfinished business to surface—issues with parents, family, society. You're strong enough now to deal with them. It's time to establish a strong identity, because there will be new pressures soon.

Rhianna was surprised to discover that age thirty-seven activated her nesting instinct:

> *After living in a succession of apartments, I've gone in with two friends to buy a Craftsman-period bungalow in a "gentrifying" part of town. It's a fixer-upper and should keep us all busy for quite some time. I realized that I could wait so long for that perfect, permanent relationship that my whole life would be gone. If I do find someone, I can sell my share of the house and move on. In the meantime, I'm accomplishing something I can point to with pride.*

Brad has encountered the question of property from the other side: "No matter how much you believe in something that you are helping to build, if someone else holds the purse strings and does not feel they should be spending their money on what you are building, they will make you 'go away,' even if that means that the item you are helping to build 'goes away' also. In this case, forever." He doesn't care for being unemployed, but he likes being available to help friends.

Later this year the nodes of the moon will return to their natal position. The moon rules your emotional life. Be prepared for some reappraisal of goals and relationships. Uranus is also changing, opposing its position in your natal chart from now until you are forty-two. This can make you very nervous unless you remember that the job of Uranus is to move you toward something new. It will bring with it a change in perception—your view of reality is going to shift, but don't worry, it's natural.

Lucile says, "There haven't been any dramatic changes in my life, but more an evolution whose direction is not yet clear."

THE BIRTHDAY

If the planets are going to be dancing through your life this year; pay them some attention. Have a moon or star-watching party. Plan a trip to the local planetarium and watch the star show. Decorate with an astrological motif and play a recording of "The Planets," the wonderful astrological tone poem by Gustav Holst, at the party.

Thirty-eight

THIS YEAR WILL CONTINUE THE MOVEMENT begun in the last. Inner conflicts may challenge you. It's time to make up your mind! You're moving into a new level of commitment. Jupiter's good vibes are behind you, the moon's nodal review is waning, and your old teacher, Saturn, is finally getting off the square and preparing to move on.

You are in good shape for tackling issues—consider joining a support group and doing some work. Learn to listen to your psyche. If you discuss your inner conflicts you'll learn something. Your destiny is pushing you, but don't let self-imposed limitations confine you. Z remembers the many beautiful California days she forced herself to spend indoors because she had to finish a script or rehearse a play. Your body is important too. Honor it!

These days, many women are having children in their forties, but for some, the later thirties will be the time to end the possibility of childbearing, either for medical reasons or because your family is complete. A ritual for the voluntary renunciation of fertility will make this transition easier. It is important to recognize that you are still in the season of the Mother, and will continue to serve her by bearing children of the mind and spirit.

Diana remembers this as the year when she really had to make the commitment to writing. Her first novel sold at last, and the same year she was laid off from her job writing educational materials. In her Christmas letter, she wrote, "It is hard to express what it means to have all those dreams, and all the hours stolen from other things, validated at last—I feel like a girl whose illicit lover of many years has finally married her."

THE BIRTHDAY

The rest of your life is busy enough, and it may be about to get busier. Take this opportunity to relax. Don't throw a big party this year. Instead, why not ask someone you love to go away with you for the weekend to a hotel or spa, or camping in the nearest national park, whichever you'll find most relaxing.

Thirty-nine

THIS YEAR IS A TIME TO WORK on our personal identity by asking questions. What is the purpose that defines us? Self-knowledge leads to self-esteem, which is what will get us through the anxiety that comes with facing forty. If we don't get on with the process of soul development we risk depression. Making our souls is the starwork of our lifetimes.

For Diana, this was not only the year when her first novel was published, but the time when her developing work as a priestess led to a formal ordination. But certainty does not always come so easily. Aurielle comments, "I don't feel anywhere near that old. So much of me still seems 'childlike' and undeveloped. I still don't have a true bead on my own instincts and feelings as I thought I would at this age. Actually, the only time I really remember that I'm thirty-nine is when I'm with women much younger than me and hear my own long-gone angst fall from their lips. . . ."

As we frenetically pursue our destinies, we need to remember that the soul transcends all these changes. As Lyn says, "I've begun to believe that storytelling is for the young, the old, and for those who get paid to do it. Those of us in the middle are generally too tired to tell a good story. Unless, of course, there are drinks involved." It will be hard, for this is a time when many of us are so submerged in work we hardly have time to think. Force yourself to come up for air from time to time and look at the stars.

Z recalls:

> *I don't even remember my thirty-ninth year. I was so caught up in meetings, writing books, having a lover, going out, dealing with my vision of my destiny. When my mother died that year I was totally depressed for a while. After that I was sunk in denial. But eventually I had to deal with the deep changes that a mother's death brings. There was nobody between me and death. It frightened me. When your mother dies you have to be an adult.*

THE BIRTHDAY

This year may be too busy for storytelling, but you can make time for it on your birthday. Invite friends with whom you can truly relax and load a table with yummy finger food. Lounge on cushions in a circle and pass a horn or large goblet of something delicious. As the horn comes to each woman in the circle, she has to tell a story, preferably something with humor. It can be about herself or about you, or about both of you. What's the funniest thing that happened to you during the past decade? Laughter is healing medicine.

Forty

IF YOU CAN'T TRUST ANYONE OVER THIRTY, forty is unthinkable. You are thirty-something forever, and then suddenly it's the big 4-0! Many women lose their cool over this. Forty was not meant for sissies! The best way to handle reaching this age is to surrender to its demands. The urge to change has been growing in you—now take a breath and just do it!

By this time, many of us have to deal with the needs of aging parents. Inevitably we start to think about the latter part of life. As Lyn observes, "I've learned that no matter if I think I've aged, my parents *have* aged. It's my turn to make sure that they are well provided for." This is good. Contemplating the future gives meaning to the present. Time reveals the superficialities and deems them worthless, makes you think about values. Physical changes are also beginning to remind you the time is passing. You are married to this body for life, but by now you may have realized that you and your body are maturing in different ways.

By now, as Aurielle comments, "My body has discouraged me. Or more accurately, I've discouraged it. Every day it looks flabbier, fatter, less appealing. I spent my young ugly ducklinghood waiting to grow into a swan and I must have missed it, or, more importantly, waited instead of making it happen myself, because now, this body is hard to love."

Just about the time when the soul is really taking off, we realize that our bodies are going to stay on the ground. After forty, the beloved body, giver of so much pleasure and meaning, will never be in such good shape again. Don't panic. Physical aging is natural—consider the alternative! And there are compensations. As Lyn puts it, "I'd love a bit more energy, but I wouldn't want to go back to the economics of youth."

The pressure to seek meaning in your life increases as Uranus, the great Changer, opposes its natal position in your chart. As Helen says:

> *I never thought being forty would feel so strange. It comes with a sense of panic as I realize how fast the first third of my life has come and gone. What shall I do during this middle third? . . . I stand on what feels like the plain of my life, looking back to see what I have done and knowing I have to keep moving to the mountains on the horizon, not quite sure if I am going in the right direction. I thought by forty you would have all the answers. I realized that all forty did was ask whether I had all the right questions.*

The dissatisfaction and restlessness you may be feeling at forty should push you toward some decisions. Your purpose may not change, but at this point, the manner in which it is expressed probably will.

Z remembers:

When I turned forty, I moved from Los Angeles to the San Francisco Bay Area. I had loved L.A.—the balmy winters, the smell of flowers, which sometimes managed to overwhelm the exhaust fumes. But I was having trouble breathing. There were daily announcements about smog levels, warnings not to let kids go outside to play. Then my beloved dog Ilona died at the age of ten of lung cancer. That did it. I was not going to be next.

I drove up to Oakland to visit a friend and looked around for a new home. The very first house I looked at had a fruiting tree in the backyard. It was a sister to the one I had had in L.A. So we moved, and of course, in the new place, everything changed. The purpose of my life was still to bring the Goddess back into women's consciousness. But I realized that by publishing books about my ideas I could reach many more. So I stopped teaching on a regular basis and devoted myself to writing full time.

THE BIRTHDAY

Fortieth birthday parties can range from small and intimate, like Lyn's sunrise observance from a hot tub in Death Valley, drinking absinthe with some close friends, to an all-out birthday bash, like Aldyth's blowout in a suite at the Marriott.

*I dressed in a tight red vinyl dress and claimed to be "One Hundred Years Old, so I can do whatever the **** I want!" We danced to Iggy Pop and Bowie, and the party ran until dawn. We spent the last couple of hours just talking about magick and love and social politics. On the way out of the hotel, three of us were taking stuff to the car, and an ambulance driver called out to us how great we looked. Earlier, I'd been explaining to K exactly what "Glam" is, and as we walked in the pale early morning light, our faces only slightly smudged, our hair and clothes nearly perfect, I turned to him and said, "That's Glam!" Or maybe he said it to me. It was a flawless moment!*

For many, the stress of turning forty is something to be met head-on with a celebration of what you've got and what you've achieved. Make the most of it. Get out your scrapbooks and photo collection. Invite the people who've been important in your life to celebrate what you've done together. Turning forty is not a doom, it's a doorway. Bring out the champagne and toast both the past and the future.

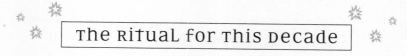

The Ritual for This Decade

CHANGING THE WORLD

In our thirties, we have the ambition and the energy to change the world. Now, when we've finished our training and are settled into the work of our Second Destiny, is the time to apply our skills to some noble purpose. Rebels in their twenties are full of idealism but have trouble focusing their energies. A decade later, we have both street smarts and resources. Ritual is not a substitute for action—think of it rather as a tool that will help you to apply power in order to produce results.

Of course "changing the world" is a pretty general statement. What, exactly, do we want to make different? Until we have a purpose, there is no point in expending energy. In each generation there are things that need changing—we've lived through the War on Poverty and the War on Drugs, marches for civil rights and marathons to raise money for breast cancer research, protests for sexual freedom and against sex discrimination. We can find problems in plenty just by turning on the six o'clock news. But some problems are more compelling than others. Each of us needs to find a cause that resonates to our depths.

Your cause may be social or economic, a health issue, or a political problem, but environmental issues are, unfortunately, always with us. The ritual structure presented here can be adapted for any issue, but ecology will serve as a useful example.

Many are familiar with the saying, "Think globally, act locally." Start by identifying an ecological problem in your area. Air or water pollution, the inner city or urban sprawl—if your region doesn't have something that needs fixing let us know, we'd like to move there! The second step is research. Get good solid information on the sources of the problem and the arguments around its solution. Ecology centers, local government, the Sierra Club, and other environmental organizations are all good resources.

At this point, you can of course go directly to action. But in our experience, doing some ritual work first will help you to engage the resources of the spirit, so that when you do get busy, you will act from your center. You can work alone, or you can gather a group who are all interested in the same issue to do both the research and the ritual.

The summary that follows is one way to do such a ritual—use it as is, or as a model for creating your own.

Begin by creating an altar. The creative effort of putting the pieces together is actually part of the spiritual work. Physically arranging symbolic items helps you to organize them mentally as well. Having something to focus on during the ritual occupies the surface mind so that your unconscious is free to work. Be aware that in seeking to change the world you are also changing yourself, placing yourself in harmony with the forces of growth and renewal. Whatever the results of your ritual and the action that follows, you yourself will be more focused and integrated afterward.

You can use a table, or build a multistage altar with boxes. Cover the whole with a cloth in an appropriate color—blue for water issues, white for air, earth-brown for most other problems. Experiment with the arrangement of symbols. On one side of the altar place items relating to the problem—books or a scrapbook with articles and photos, a map of the area, a jar of contaminated water, or a plate of earth. If, for instance, the problem you're addressing is a trashed stream, include a piece of trash from the streambed and a jar of the water. On the other side, place symbols of the desired situation—a picture of the way the place used to look, or a similar natural environment, a proposal or legal decisions about clean-up of this or similar sites. In a central position, place an image of the Earth Goddess (the online company Mythic Images has a very nice Millennial Gaia; a Venus of Willendorf statuette is also very effective), a globe, or an image of the Earth as seen from space. Before it, set four candles, black, green, white, and red.

Cleanse the space where you will be working by sweeping counterclockwise, smudging with sage, and making any other preparations you wish. Sit down in front of your altar in a balanced and comfortable position. Breathe slowly and deeply, seeking your center, extending awareness of your connection with the earth below. If you are working with others, ask, "Why have you come here?" Then you, or each of you, states what the problem is.

Light the first, black, candle. Say, "This is what has been..."

Describe the different aspects of the hazard. After each statement describe the desired change. For example:

"Where waters are dirty—Let them be clean!"

"Where waters are opaque—Let them run clear!"

"Where waters are turgid—Let them swiftly flow!"

and so forth. Keep repeating these affirmations, building in intensity, and climaxing with the refrain:

Lady, bring the change we (or I) see—

As we/I will, so mote it be!

When you have finished, take a deep breath and light the green candle. Say, "This is what shall be."

Now, you are ready for the meditation. You may find it useful to put on a tape of drumming or woodland sounds. If you are working with others, explain that the goal is to visualize the place as it is, and then to transform it with your imagination until you can clearly see it as it ought to be. When you have done that, visualize light sparkling on the water, light that coalesces until you are looking at the spirit of the stream. Speak to the spirit, ask for her help and inspiration in the work you want to do, promise that you will honor her.

Now close your eyes and do it. When you can "see" the spirit, or sense her presence in some way, ask if she has any advice on how you can address the problem, or anything she wants you to do. Wait a few moments for an answer to come to you.

When you are finished (time the tape to end after five minutes), open your eyes and light the white candle, saying, "This is the spirit that will inspire us/me!"

Now, fill a goblet or chalice with clear water. Let each person present lift the glass, describe the action she will take, drink, and pass it on. When you have finished, light the red candle, and say, "This is what we/I will do!"

Take a few moments to review and impress upon your memory what you have experienced and learned (as soon after the ritual as you can, write it down). Thank Earth Mother and the spirit of the stream, blow out your candles, and dismantle the altar. If you can, take some of its elements and make a smaller altar that you can keep up while you are working on the problem. Before you go out to clear trash or talk to authorities, light the candles for a few moments and ask the spirit for help.

AGES 41 TO 50

Crisis and Crown

HERE COME THE FORTIES! Are they fabulous or frightening, a
time of crisis or a time to claim our crowns? For many, the
fourth decade includes the most active and productive years
yet. We have survived the emotional traumas of our younger years,
but our bodies are still relatively flexible and strong. We know what we
want, and we're not afraid to go after it. In the middle of this decade,
however, the planets may bring us a period of crisis that forces us to
re-evaluate our goals.

In our forties, women move beyond the archetype of the Mother
to that of the Queen. We are well into the Second Destiny—working
hard on projects, making our dreams real. By now we are moving
steadily up the career ladder. We've been around long enough to
become senior staff, authorities. Women in particular should pay
attention to the implications. We have the power—we need to find
the courage to use it.

FATE DATES FOR AGES 41 TO 50

Age 42 ♆ □ ♆ Neptune squares self
Uranus opposes self
- Turning point in vision
- Rapid reorientation of goals, spirituality, friends
- Midlife crisis!

Ages 42–46 ♀ □ ♀ Pluto squares self
- Intensifies transformation
- Time for introspection, regeneration
- Low income for creative people
- New patterns; don't panic!

Ages 44–46 ♄ ☌ ♄ Saturn opposes self
- Ah, the return of ambition!
- Time to tie up loose ends
- Relax, enjoy a quiet time, but deal with whatever comes up
- Missed childhood? Have a second childhood now

Age 48 ♃ ☌ ♃ Jupiter returns
- New potential for growth, stability
- New career goals, further study
- Courage rises, take risks
- If children are leaving nest, use opportunities to develop own interests
- Men deal with emotional side

♄ ⊼ ♄ Saturn quincunx
- Outer identity challenges inner

Age 50 ♄ △ ♄ Saturn trines self
- Integration of opposites
- Accept next stage of life
- Vitality resurfaces

Ages 50–52 Asteroid Chiron returns
- Mental flexibility

Until very recently, only men had a personal destiny. Women's energy went into fulfilling the species destiny, bearing and raising children, and it wore us out by the time we reached fifty. We moved directly from the Age of the Mother to that of the Crone. But the women who struggled for freedom and civil rights during the previous century opened the door for us to exercise our sovereignty. We stand on their shoulders, and we should never forget the debt we owe them.

But the struggle continues. Average salaries for men are still higher than for women. Sexual harassment in the workplace continues, and we are still wrestling with the problem of how to work in what used to be a man's world without being forced to adopt masculine roles and values. Until both men and women can be nurturing or aggressive, competitive or cooperative as the situation demands, neither will be free.

In our forties, we may well be in a position in which we not only have to deal with such problems, but have the authority to make changes. Busy as we are, it's important to step back from time to time, take a deep breath, and think hard about what we are doing and why.

Forty-one

WE SLIP INTO AGE FORTY-ONE STILL WORKING on integrating the changes from the previous decade. But fortunately the planets will be giving us a break about now from the constant assault of decisions about changing careers, lifestyles, countries, relationships, or even identity. Instead, we need to take this opportunity to release and explore the person we are now.

As adolescents, we were still learning how to survive, which sometimes required suppressing elements of our personality in order to fit in. We followed orders, turned resentments in upon ourselves—ate our own flesh, so to speak, because we were powerless. But now we are becoming Queens, and we can let it all come roaring out!

Aldyth comments:

> *[Being in my forties] definitely feels better than thirty. On one
> level I feel the press of time, but on another, I feel healthier and
> more secure than possibly I ever have before. I feel very much like
> me. I am much calmer about things, even though I take them just
> as seriously. I finally learned to meditate, which has been incred-
> ibly enriching! And because I am physically healthier I am
> exploring physical things that I hadn't before, like camping, and
> learning belly dance.*

Life has prepared us to rule over our own areas of expertise, our
own domains. Now is the time to nurture traits that we've been
repressing, to meet hidden needs. The next five years will be a time
of fulfillment.

THE BIRTHDAY

The energy of this age should be expressed actively. You've got it all
together, baby, so dance!

Aldyth remembers her forty-first birthday:

> *About twelve friends and I went to a Japanese restaurant for
> dinner, where the host kept pouring us more sake. Afterward
> about half of us went to this amazing glam club called Glitz, to
> see Blue Period play and generally behave outrageously. After
> that, we went to Assimilate to dance some more. What was
> bizarre about the evening was that earlier that day someone I
> cared about had ripped into me, and one of my girlfriends came
> to my support. I considered canceling going out, but ultimately
> decided I wasn't going to let that person ruin my life or my day. It
> was worth it, 'cause I realized then that she cared for me as
> much as I did for her, and that was kind of the start of us as a
> couple.*

Forty-two

THIS YEAR BRINGS US ANOTHER COSMIC EVENT. Neptune the Dreamer and Conceptualizer is squared with its own natal point. This means we will reach a turning point in our vision. Uranus the great Disrupter is now moving into opposition to his position on our birth chart. We need to brace ourselves for a midlife crisis! At forty-two, we find that we are losing our old ideals, a shift that will continue over the next year. For some, this loss of our old worldview brings depression, but hold on and stay open to new ideas. Dream life grows more active now. In the depths, new values and desires are stirring. If we work to bring them into consciousness, we'll find ourselves with a new and more appropriate philosophy of life.

To add to the stress, this year wealth-loving Pluto also squares its own natal point. Pluto stirs up issues relating to sex and death, so our souls get a deep cleansing at the same time as our ideals are changing. This process will take approximately until you are forty-six. The early forties can be difficult, but they don't have to be. The Fates weave our personal destinies into the tapestry that tells the story of our generation. If you are already in harmony with the changes the stars are bringing, you'll have a great year.

Sue, for instance, enjoys being forty-two. As she says:

> *I feel I can stop worrying about what other people think of me. I'm still in good shape—physically healthy—but not a "kid" anymore. I'm less willing to be pushed around or bullied by people because I don't believe they know more or have more life experience than I do. I no longer view others as having a "right" to be leaders while I am the follower. My thirties were a much better time in my life than my twenties, and the twenties were better than the teens. So far, my forties are even better than the previous decade. If this keeps up, the fifties will be fabulous, and by my sixties or seventies I'll be close to achieving the perfect life. Since family history and heredity make it likely that I'll see my one hundredth birthday, I think the stories are going to get better and better as I age. I'm looking forward to it.*

THE BIRTHDAY

For your forty-second birthday, have a party for your dreams. Celebrate alone, or with a few other people close to you in age. Invite Neptune to the party. Decorate with blues and purples and an oceanic theme. Play the "Neptune" movement from Holst's *The Planets,* Debussy's *La Mer,* or a tape of ocean sounds. If you are living on one of the coasts, go to the beach or spend the weekend in a seaside cottage.

After you've had a good seafood dinner and blown out your birthday candles, kick back with a bottle of good wine or some soothing herbal tea and let your mind float free on the music. Ask your unconscious what it really wants, and imagine that you are dropping that question into the depths of the sea. As it drifts down, down, let your mind drift. Keep a notepad handy, and write down any thoughts that come to you.

Forty-three

DURING THIS TRANSITION, ALL POSSIBILITIES are being restructured. The good news is that the new goals will be clarified fairly quickly. New patterns are being established, but it may take awhile for the results to become apparent. Creative people, in particular, may have to endure a period of hovering on the edge of success. The universe does not turn on a dime. Movements that affect a whole generation interact with those affecting individuals.

Don't panic. Take this opportunity to re-evaluate your life. Leave some time for introspection, recuperation, and regeneration. There is no point in racing through this time and scattering your energy. Don't deny this important turning point. If you don't deal with your issues now, when the stars are behind you, unfinished business will hamper your ability to take advantage of the good energy that's coming. Opportunities appropriate to your unique needs will gradually present themselves, and you can synchronize your own development with that of your generation.

This sea change of the soul takes a long time—it's a period of daily discovery. If you have found a philosophy that gives you comfort, look for its heart. Try to sense the way that all beings are interconnected in the web of life. Explore many solutions. Spirituality is only good if it has some common sense and improves your quality of life.

It can be a year of contradictions. Deborah comments that she is "forty-three, sometimes going on six, sometimes six hundred. . . . When I'm moving well, it feels great [to be this age]. I am strong, powerful, in control. When the joints ache, it just plain hurts. I'm getting a better grip on my limits. I don't overschedule myself so much anymore, and I get more done."

It can also be a year of new responsibilities. When Marion Zimmer Bradley decided to dissolve the umbrella organization that was sheltering the Darkmoon women's circle and several other new groups, Diana had to make the decision to come out from behind her shadow as a priestess, and lead the reorganization of the group as the Fellowship of the Spiral Path.

Z remembers:

> *At the beginning of my forties I started the Laughing Goddess coven in the Bay Area with about seventeen women. For a while, it was heaven. Down in Los Angeles, I had been leading public rituals, but here in northern California there were a lot of groups for people to choose from, so the circles were by invitation only. The truth was, I was tired from ten years of leading big circles without a microphone. Here, I found a stronger focus on the personal than the political. I still talked about the importance of reclaiming the Goddess, but it was also a time to explore lesbian identity.*

THE BIRTHDAY

This is not the year to have a big party. Instead, get away from the distractions of home and family. You can go camping or to a motel, it doesn't matter—the point is to hang out for a couple of days without the distraction of other living people around. It's the ancestors who will be your guests at this birthday.

When night has fallen, light three candles in holders next to your little birthday cake. The black one is for the universe and the cauldron of creation; the red for your own physical life, maturing now like a fine wine; the white for the spirit world from which you came and to which you will return. Burn some incense, especially frankincense and myrrh. If you are inside, open a window. Open the doors of your spirit as well.

As you light the last candle, say something like:

> *Ancestor spirits, winging near—*
> *Let the fair winds bear you here.*
> *Sweet scent persuade you to abide,*
> *Settle softly at my side. . . .*

Fall silent, and open your awareness. Do you feel a presence near you? Do you have a sense who it might be? Talk to the spirit about your life, your hopes, your needs. Now light a candle on your little cake and invite the spirits to share it with you with words such as:

> *With the cake that's waiting there,*
> *The sweetness of my life I share.*
> *The love we share to me you've drawn,*
> *We share the love you have passed on.*

Cut a piece of cake for the ancestors and set it aside. Then cut another for yourself and eat it.

If you have a tarot deck, draw three cards at random and look at them. What wisdom do the spirits have for you?

Then go to sleep, alone. Prophetic dreams may come, so be ready to record them.

Forty-four

HERON HAS A GOOD STORY about the forty-fourth birthday:

> *It was March in Connecticut, and my mom's birthday. I was*
> *five at the time. March dumped oodles of snow on our small town*

*and I loved it. Snow is magical when you're young and even now
that first snowfall, even if the flakes melt before touching the
ground—it's still magic. My dad kissed my mom good-bye and
went outside to drive off to work. . . . I watched him stamping out
something on our 6' by 9' concrete porch. . . . When I realized what
it was I thought it was so neat—he waved and left for work leaving two three-foot high numbers stamped into the snow. "Forty-
four" was written out in a small quick action with a mountain of
love behind it. . . .*

*Dad's been gone for six years. I'm in Virginia now and talk to
my mom in Connecticut once a week, see her every couple of
months. I've got different spiritual beliefs from either of them,
bedded but never wedded, connect with the same sex and won't
ever have kids, but the small gesture he made for her will always
stay with me. . . . I suppose being forty-four is a good time. Life
sucks living with chronic migraines, but those enforced quiet
times give me room to work out stories in my head and the muses
have been very generous. I know who I am more than any other
time in my life, and that too is a blessing. I don't have the body of
a twenty-two-year-old, but the wisdom has more than made up
for it. I may be cash poor, but I am rich in friends.*

In our mid-forties, we are saying good-bye to our foolish youth.
Saturn is now moving into opposition to his natal position. No matter
how uncertain we feel, from here on out, the universe expects us to be
grown-ups. It's time to stop blaming our problems on our childhoods
and take full responsibility for our actions. On the plus side, we should
be ready for it! All the soul-searching we have been doing since we
turned forty will come in handy now. We need to turn our emotions
toward forgiveness and love, to bless those who brought us into the
world, whatever their faults. At forty-four, we've experienced enough
to understand that they were doing the best they could, just as we are.

At this turning point, unfinished business may resurface. We have
to deal with it in order to go forward. Old feelings of inadequacy are
challenged by developing ambition. Life cannot be lived for the moment

only; it must have depth, truth, and meaning. This isn't always easy—getting a handle on it may take all year.

Solange comments:

> *In turning forty-four, I somehow feel more "mature" than I have felt yet in my life. I feel that everything I have done somehow has led up to this moment (though it's only been about four days since I turned forty-four), and that it is very important to me to remember my spirituality, and the importance it has played in my life and will continue to play. I also feel that I can finally deal with some of my self-esteem issues, like losing weight permanently, and that it will truly be a "last diet" for me, not the yo-yo-ing I've been experiencing. I somehow feel "equipped" to deal with things now that I couldn't before.*

THE BIRTHDAY

Okay—you're all grown up now. So prove it. Make a list of the people who have hurt you and how. Allow each memory to surface. Contemplate it—bring the pain into your awareness, and then let it go. If you are still in contact with the individual, write a letter explaining how you felt, and forgiving them. If someone was not aware how she had hurt you, this will contribute to her spiritual development. If she did know, your forgiveness may ease her pain.

Hold the list over a baking tray, and set fire to it. Throw the ashes into running water, or let the wind carry them away. Say:

> *Hurt and hatred, resentment and envy,*
> *All pain from the past, I release you now—*
> *Begone, begone, begone!*

Then light your birthday candles. With each one, name some quality that you want to bring into your life.

Forty-five

ONGRATULATIONS! AT FORTY-FIVE, you are at the halfway mark in your reign. This is a turning point. Now you can look back and evaluate what you have done so far. If there has been a pattern in your life you will be able to see it now. Saturn is still in opposition to his natal position in your chart, and will stay there until next year. Do you remember what it was like to be fifteen? Get ready to experience some of those feelings again.

At this point, many of us begin to get restless and look for other ways to do what we've been doing. Or we throw caution to the winds and begin something brand-new. In the old days people called this the "midlife crisis." It caused depression and disappointment. They looked back at the "road not taken" and yearned for a better life. Venus wakes up and shows her power, causing men to run off with younger secretaries or buy sexy sports cars they can't afford, or in some cases, "come out" as gay. Women walk out on their families, take male lovers or decide they are lesbians, or get depressed and attempt suicide.

It doesn't have to be that way. Midlife anxiety can be a wake-up call, not a warning. Mindful living allows us to anticipate the changing energy and use it. It's hard work to be a human being. The fact that we have made it this far is a victory, not a tragedy. Take out your old dreams and dust them off. The best is yet to come.

Marina is trying to treat "midlife crisis" as a challenge:

> Sometimes I wake up at night with my heart pounding, wondering if I am going to have enough money to get through the year. I used to dig out my bank statements for reassurance, but that just made me worry more. I finally decided to make my insomnia useful, and I've started a novel. It's pretty much stream of consciousness, and no one will ever read it, but it relieves my feelings, and after a few pages I get tired and then I can sleep again.

Roy comments:

> *Work is hard and it makes me feel old. My knees creak when I*
> *kneel too long and my bones seem to crack a lot more often. But*
> *the people I work with are real nice and that part of work I really*
> *enjoy. . . . When not at work, I feel like I am young and free. I have*
> *always had the philosophy of, "One does not have to grow up, one*
> *just needs to be responsible at the proper times." And with that*
> *in mind, life is lived like it is one big adventure. Fun is normal.*
> *Sometimes my body puts limitations on what I can do, but the*
> *restrictions are minor and I am not afraid to "go for it." At forty-*
> *five, I know that I am well over half way through the adventure,*
> *but I don't think that makes me old. I feel very young at heart*
> *with a lot to look forward to. I look at other people my age and*
> *they seem to be "older than me." I have to feel sorry for them, '-*
> *'cause life doesn't really have to be that hard.*

Take a good hard look at your life. Do you feel imprisoned or excited by your occupation? It is not the amount of money you made that's the real pay-off for the time you have spent working, but the satisfaction, the wisdom you have gained. If you don't like your work, ask yourself what you would rather be doing. At this point in their lives, some people switch careers, go back to school to get a different degree.

For Diana, the mid-forties were also a time of spiritual unfolding: "I started a rune-study class just as I turned forty-five, for which the material arrived so easily it felt like a 'download,' and the next year developed a method for doing oracle work which is now being used not only here but in other parts of the U.S. and Europe as well."

THE BIRTHDAY

On this birthday, let the soul work you've been doing be reflected by getting rid of old baggage on the physical plane. Clean out your closets, your garage, your cupboards, and hold a rummage giveaway. You've just found that dress you bought for your twenty-fifth birthday? You know you'll never get into it again, and it wouldn't fit the person you are now anyway. And what about the scarf that Aunt Nancy gave you for Christmas two years ago? You're not going to like it any better two years from now.

If it's worn out or broken, throw it away. If it's still useful, set it out, and invite all your friends over. Instead of having them give you presents, give things away. As you munch on birthday cake, tell the story of each item—where you got it, what it meant to you. Donate whatever's left over to charity.

Forty-six

B Y THE END OF THIS YEAR SATURN will be moving out of opposition to his natal point. You've had your wake-up call. At last you can see what lies ahead. You're not finished—a new chapter in your life is just beginning. It's a great relief to feel your oats again. Now it's time to make a slow, comfortable, but definite change. For creative people, class is over, and the hard times are ending.

How things develop now may depend on what you did during your First Destiny, or how well you dealt with the issues that Uranus, the great changer, dredged up from your unconscious. No single prediction can cover everybody. Whether it's a blessing or a curse, we do have free will. The universe builds the house, but it is up to us to do the interior decoration. To succeed, we must use the gifts we've been given to solve the problems before us. That's the nature of organic life.

During the mid-forties, those whose childhoods were cut short or blighted for any reason can recapture them. Those who shirked adulthood and extended their adolescence can shift from self-involvement to taking responsibility for their own choices. Whichever extreme we went to, now is the time to balance it. This is a time for reversals. Spin slowly, but snap out of it!

Sharon finds in her forty-sixth year a new awakening:

The years of my life have created an internal tapestry with a
gently evolving design. I am still weaving in details not yet fully

*imagined as I open myself to the fates. Some of the original
pastel pattern was the result of being raised by eccentric yet
loving Catholic parents during the baby boom era. It really came
to life when I realized that I could reach for that needle and select
new and vibrantly dyed threads! I stitched in jewel-toned swirls
of new music and sacraments, new cultures, philosophies, and
lifestyles. The births of my daughters were celebrated by deepening colors. New textures emerged as generations were braided
together through me.*

*At forty-six I feel ready to give birth to myself once again. I am
choosing new threads that must stretch farther than ever before,
connecting me to the world in a new way. I am weaving more
environmental and community service, more political action into
my personal story. I spent years expanding from my heart
chakra upward. Now I am more grounded and consciously living
in my body, my temple.*

*At forty-six there are fewer fine golden threads in my mane,
and the waxing white ones are outrageous as they stand up like
antennae, strong and free, not conforming to my wishes to look
groomed. Seems like a symbolic forecast to me. I am looking forward to my wisdom years.*

But not everyone has the same experience. Linda says, "I celebrated my last birthday by getting a massage which I needed as a
reminder that living in my body isn't all aches and pains. I feel like
I've come to the halfway point of my life with very little to show for
it. I've learned that I can't rely on anything to be secure. I'm entering
a new mysterious stage of life at age forty-six with a story that's still
unfolding."

THE BIRTHDAY

As a part of your search for balance, on this birthday, take a little time
to analyze your life pattern. Then do the opposite! If you were always
the one who took care of everybody else, then become a child again on
your birthday. Go to the zoo or the beach. Play party games. Blow up bal-

loons and eat lots of candy. Put six, instead of forty-six, candles on your cake.

If, on the other hand, you now realize that you've been too self-involved, spend this birthday doing something for others. Do you have a friend who hasn't been getting out much lately? Tell her you need company and ask her to share your birthday. Cook a scrumptious meal for all your friends. If you can't give back, give forward. Find some organization that needs volunteers.

Forty-seven

THIS YEAR WE CONTINUE TO FINISH UP the starwork of the past two years. The push that Uranus gave you has had its effect and is starting you off on a new direction. Now you have to deal with the consequences of that burst of energy. Now is when midlife crisis can really settle in. But now, the end is in sight. It's a good thing, too, because your body is changing as well as your psyche. The deep hormonal rearrangement ordained by nature is on its way, and many women who have not already done so are moving into perimenopause, a condition uncomfortably reminiscent of pre-adolescence. Although a thorough physical examination is always a good idea, don't let these first changes alarm you—Nature is just ringing a warning bell.

This does not, of course, mean that we stop being interested in sex, but it has to have soul. Unfortunately, just at the point when women may be looking for some meaningful romance, men our age are beginning to slow down. Some lose not only their hair, but their libido. Both sexes fight against aging. Crones and cronies alike go into denial.

But something else is happening as well. At the same time as we realize that our bodies are moving in the direction of mortality, we become more aware of the blissful immortality of our souls. The soul matures rather than aging, unlike its partner, the body. We always knew this in theory, but now we have to face it. When we were born, body and soul were both infant. Their ways are parting now.

Moondancer says, "Personal health is a lot more important to me this year than it has been in the past. While I haven't exactly abused my body, I haven't particularly taken good care of it either, and it tells: hypertension, diabetes, fibromyalgia.... I'm changing things with my worldview to allow me to take better care of me, and not be so worried about the rest of the world."

At forty-seven we are really taking charge of our own development. From Gabriele in Germany comes this account:

> If I see life as a hike, I am nowadays on the hilltop. I am able to look back to realize how the course has been. There have been sharp bits, making me stumble and tumble, experience that hurt me, and damage which has healed. The impassible parts of the way strengthened me. There have been parts where I lost my way, false decisions, wrong ways, detours which could perhaps have been avoided. These wrong ways and detours gave me experience and knowledge. There have been marvelous parts of the way, meadows to rest in, streams to quench my thirst, people who became real friends, moments filled with happiness and love. These parts of the way are my precious treasure of memories. That is the past. I don't want to miss it, but I have not got any need to get back to my earlier life.
>
> I am on the hilltop of life, therefore I can see into the future: the descent is more comfortable than the first part of the way has been, because I can see in the distance my destination, the river, which takes me back to the eternal ocean. I can see not only the end of life, but also the way in front of me. Again there will be sharp bits, but I have the power to overcome these difficulties. Surely, from time to time I will deviate from my way, making side trips to gain new experience and knowledge. I am looking forward gladly to the good parts of the way.

THE BIRTHDAY

This is a birthday to celebrate with close and trusted friends. Go to a spa together for a massage and sauna, or have a "Body Time" evening at home. Set candles around the room and put on soft music. If you have a hot tub, take a good long soak. Lay out towels and different scents of massage oil. Take turns working on each other.

Have food and drink that you really like. After your friends have toasted you, offer your own toast—to your body! Say something like:

"I'd like to offer a toast to my faithful body, my truest mate and partner, that has awakened with me every morning for so many years, and gone to sleep with me every evening. My faithful servant, my dearest lover—glory and thanks to you, dearest body, for keeping me breathing, my heart beating, my muscles moving. In gratitude, I pledge to take care of you for the rest of our journey, that we may both live to a healthy old age! Blessed be!"

Then, get on with the party!

Forty-eight

JUST WHEN WE THOUGHT WE HAD EVERYTHING figured out, there's a new cosmic kick in the equation! Jupiter the Luck-bringer returns to his natal position for the fourth time, bringing opportunities, potential, and growth. What more do we want? This is a fine year—the fog has lifted, the funk has passed. We discover the joy of having gotten this far. Everything makes so much more sense now.

We need to take advantage of this energy to grow. Jupiter's influence will stimulate interest in travel, study, and career development. Courage rises, giving us the impetus to take risks. But we need to take care not to get carried away—make time for meditation, so the soul doesn't get left behind. Jupiter's energy affects every aspect of our lives. Long-standing patterns, whether they are relationships or careers, can be threatened if they have not been re-examined earlier.

At the same time, Saturn is in the quincunx position—just the other side of opposition. We begin to look outward, and our sense of identity is challenged by the world. We may become more assertive, but inner values have to be challenged and focused to support that action.

Diana remembers, "My involvement with the physical world

expressed itself in a new interest in gardening. I attacked the front yard with passion, getting rid of the ivy that had overgrown it, and putting in native plants and herbs, an activity that released excess energy and promoted growth at the same time."

Debra writes:

> *Physically I feel young and beautiful. My heart is calm and at peace, yet my spirit is wild and free. I have learned that although life isn't always beautiful, it is made up of many beautiful moments. And then I learned that even the not-so-beautiful moments really are, that they were necessary in making me the divine woman I am today. I have learned that it feels better to forgive than to get even, and sometimes when something doesn't turn out "perfect" it really is, because it is how it was planned by a higher force. I have learned that you can't be too passionate, love too hard, or care too deeply. It really is okay. And no matter how devastated you can become by events, you can rise up, like the phoenix, from the ashes, but it's not easy. Most important, I have learned to love myself and laugh at myself.*

At this age, many women whose earlier years were dominated by the needs of their families are realizing it is time to take care of themselves. This new awareness can lead to ambivalent feelings about earlier life choices, and relationships with partners who are not ready for change can suffer. Nonetheless, this is a healthier response than that of those women who try to hang on to outdated roles. It is time to let go gracefully and let your children lead their own lives. Either way, you need balance in your life.

We need to be aware of what's going on with the men in our lives as well. Now, as male hormones diminish, many men are for the first time able to deal with repressed emotions. The man from Mars has emigrated to Venus. If this kind of emotionally emancipated man falls in love, it's a major event. He may say, "I feel as if this is the first time," and he's right. Nature has finally mellowed him into the kind of man we've wanted since our twenties. Things have changed.

Ages 41 to 50 * *Crisis and Crown*

The Birthday

Welcome Jupiter's jovial influence with another "royal party." Decorate with blue, play the "Jupiter" movement from Holst's *The Planets.* At this party, you are the Queen. Let your friends give you a crown and a throne. Jupiter brings joy—share the joy that is coming into your life this year by starting a kiss that travels around your circle of friends until it returns to you again.

Since you are the Queen, you can choose your consort for the evening, and command your friends to entertain you. It's also your responsibility to share your luck with them. Wish for Health, Wealth, and Wisdom for all. Distribute largesse—golden coins (of chocolate covered with foil). Give each guest a lucky charm.

Forty-nine

A GOOD LUCK STREAK FLOATS THROUGH THIS YEAR like a kite. We are tiptoeing into fifty, true, but our spirits have just come of age. No matter how long you live, your spirit will always have this vibrant maturity. Hopefully, your personal destiny gives you the energy to achieve what you need to do. Our works are significant at last. We find our voice, the form of expression that others will understand. Writers are doing their best work.

We also still have the stamina for a healthy, active life. Given half a chance, sexuality flowers. So this is the time to take a look at our lives. We need to examine our desires and identify what's still lacking. We should look at our sense of justice and see if there's something important we need to stand up for, refocus our mission for the second part of our Second Destiny. These are the years when we become High Queens—we should be generous. Now is the time to become a mentor to a young woman seeking to enter our field. If we share our good fortune, it will multiply.

We need to devote this year to cultivating our spirits. We should be bearing fruit at this age, achieving a noble goal. We need to take care of our physical component—our bodies—as well. By our forty-ninth year, most women who have not already started the Change are experiencing perimenopause. The first symptoms may be subtle. As Diana wrote in her Christmas letter for that year, "The spring was tense, waiting for a book payment that came in four months later than expected. That, plus pre-menopausal hormone fluctuations, lowered my productivity during the first half of the year. Then I got my money, figured out what my body was doing and started taking herbs and vitamins to compensate, and ever since have been furiously busy trying to catch up."

Fortunately, these days a great deal of information on menopause is available. Susun Weed's book *Menopausal Years* is an excellent guide to what can happen and what you can do about it.

Liadan says:

> This is the happiest period of my life so far. I am looking at my fiftieth birthday next summer as a pivotal one: all the growth I have done in my life has brought me to this point. I live each day in gratitude for my good fortune. The long years of financial struggle and trauma and emotional snarls are just memories that have lost their sting. This year I have learned that I'm a better artist than I thought. I have become more assertive and am confident and capable in a variety of areas. I am also beginning to experience a condition that some call "CRS": I am noticeably more forgetful these days. My body is changing, preparing for the Change, and I am watching carefully. I have lost over thirty pounds, and am learning healthful habits that I hope will contribute to the quality of life I experience in the future.

By the end of the forty-ninth year, we are beginning to look toward the future.

"Whyzz" reports:

> Eight weeks before my fiftieth birthday, I feel like I am coming out of a cocoon—a dark and restrictive place where the changes in me were inside, hidden, and I was bound, unable to see what

was happening. If I feel that my nest is empty since I am single now and my daughter is in college, I am also flapping my wet wings and wondering how it will feel to fly. I know that there are things that I can't do right now, unless I give up the things I am working on. So I make choices. I am content that I have choices to make, and I pour my energy into those choices.

Lee says:

Plantar fascitis has slowed me down and put a crimp in my quality of life. It has taught me to love myself and to love my feet and pay more attention to them because they still have many miles to go before I'm done in this life. . . . If I should retire from the library, I would like to get involved in healing work on some level. I like where I am today—more sure of my tomorrow and secure in knowing that the Goddess is forever at my side.

THE BIRTHDAY

The forty-ninth birthday can be an opportunity for a great adventure—Liadan reports:

I went camping for ten days with my beloved. It's what I wanted more than anything else. We explored great lava tubes with ice in their depths, canoed high mountain lakes, saw wildflowers and lodgepole pines, waterfalls and pictographs, osprey and eagles. We made gourmet meals for each other, priding ourselves on camping with comfort and class. We worked on our plans for a future together in a beautiful place.

Lee says, "I turned forty-nine at the Goddess 2000 celebration in La Honda, California. It was a memorable birthday because I was doing what I wanted to be doing with some of the most wonderful kindred spirits that I have had the privilege to be with."

If you don't travel for your birthday, have a party that reflects (or invokes) the opulence of the goddess of the harvest. Make a toast to Bona Fortuna, goddess of good luck and abundance.

Fifty

AGE FIFTY IS AN AUSPICIOUS TIME for us all. The asteroid Chiron is returning, bringing the energy of the wounded healer back to your life. He bestows upon you the ability to move between conceptual galaxies—cultures, jobs, belief systems. This is the time when you come into your own, as a manager at work or as a teacher. If you make good use of Chiron's teaching, you will do well. Find a way to pass on what you have learned—doing so will give meaning to your life and connect you more deeply to the human family.

The winds of fate will also be blowing from the direction of Saturn this year. This teacher of the laws will be trined to his position on your natal chart, which brings good luck and harmony. This is Saturn's blessing on the prime time of your life. Fifty can be a time for beginning a new adventure. As life expectancy increases, age fifty moves closer to the midpoint of the life span, which means that you are at your "peak" right now. Will this be the beginning of fulfillment, or is it all downhill from here? It's up to you.

As Muhammed Ali once said in a *Playboy* interview, "The man who views the world at 50 the same as he did at 20 has wasted 30 years of his life" (November 1975).

Barbara comments:

> When I'm talking to younger women sometimes it's like a mirror from former times. Now as I'm fifty years old I often notice that I'm stepping into another realm, where it's less important to be the best and to be on stage, to be seen in my greatness, because I know that I'm a unique being, one of many goddesses in this world, and this knowledge helps me to relax and be. I know what I'm able to do and I know about my boundaries. I still want to stretch those boundaries and open up. Thirteen years as an M.D. and thirteen years as an artist are behind me, and now I'm stepping into a new career wanting to merge those experiences. Again it's a shift, but meanwhile, shifting feels quite normal. After all that struggle, I'm no longer anxious about

saying my opinion directly and with a strong voice. . . . My body is not able to move as it did thirty years ago, but my mind is creative enough to find ways how to solve those problems and trusts at being at the right place at the right time. . . . Being my age feels great.

The sense that it's time to shift toward a more spiritual approach to life is felt by men as well as women. Marshall says, "It feels like the first half of the *work* is done, and now I can get past self-doubt and make the *real* important things happen in this incarnation."

THE BIRTHDAY

Fifty years! Half a century! It's your Golden Birthday! Whether you celebrate at home or go out to a good restaurant, have a cake with creamy frosting and five golden candles to represent your five decades. If friends want ideas for appropriate presents, something golden, such as a pendant or an astrological medallion with your birth sign, would mark the occasion. At your birthday party, wear a party crown.

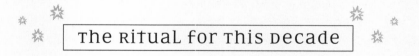

the Ritual for This Decade

FREEDOM FROM FERTILITY

By the time we reach fifty, most women are nearing the end of our fertile years. We're either in perimenopause or finished with bleeding entirely. But we're nowhere near ready to proclaim ourselves Elders. Just as beginning menstruation didn't make us adult women, stopping doesn't instantly turn us into Crones. Indeed, by this time, for many women physical fertility is no longer possible in any case, either because of a tubal ligation or a hysterectomy. Letting go of our fertility is psychological as much as physical, the beginning of a time of transformation that may take ten to fifteen years.

Nonetheless, we need to honor the beginning of this change, just as we will eventually celebrate its completion. If Nature does not clearly signal the right time for you to celebrate, choose a time in your late forties or your fifti-eth year.

In structure, this ritual can be similar to the welcome into womanhood. Begin with a ritual bath of purification—by now, you have your own distinct preferences in bath fragrances, so use them—or if the situation permits, invite your friends to soak with you in a hot tub. As you do so, think about those things in your life that you will no longer need to be concerned with—the monthly mess of menstruation, the psychological compulsion to be fertile (or to appear to be so), ways of thinking about yourself that were appropriate earlier in your life but which you are outgrowing now.

One change that many of us have noticed is in our relationship to our mothers. The pubescent girl needs to cut the cord of dependence that binds her to her mother (and the mother needs to release her). The menopausal woman needs to free herself from internalized images that bind her to out-of-date ideas about what her future will be. When our mothers went through menopause thirty or forty years ago, this change was often a farewell to sexual attractiveness. Today, it represents a new freedom.

When you have soaked long enough, get out and get dry. Use scented powder or lotion if you like, put on a comfortable garment—a silky caftan or lounging robe in any color except red, and join your guests for the party.

If one or more of your friends has already gone through menopause, she or they should first bar the way, then surround you with a group hug, and then release you into the room. The arms of your sisters are the womb of wis-domhood from which you are now being born. If you are the first of your group to go through "the Change," drop your arms to your sides and have your friends loosely tie a red ribbon around you. As you reach the door, burst it open. However you do it, when you go through the door, proclaim that this is the first day of your new life.

Sit down in a circle with plenty of your favorite food and drink. Share some of the insights you had during your soak. What are you giving up, and from what are you gaining a new freedom? In your new life, what do you hope to gain? Encourage those women who have already gone through menopause to talk about their experiences, share advice, remedies, and secrets. Will you try estrogen, or go with vitamins or vegetable phytoestrogens? How does love change when it is not connected to fertility?

Talk about the symbolism of the moon as well. Although your body will no longer bleed in response to lunar cycles, your hormones and biorhythms are still affected. You now have the opportunity to explore a new kind of moon cycle in which each full moon gives you an opportunity for spiritual fertility. Whether or not you have borne children, the time for that kind of physical relationship to the young is ended. Now you can mother children (your own or those borne by others) in the spirit.

When the intensity of the discussion slackens, your friends may offer you gifts. The first thing you open, however, should be a ring, presented by your friends or purchased as an act of self-realization by yourself. The pubescent girl wore a ring with a red stone to symbolize her blood flow, so your ring should be some other color. An amethyst would be appropriate, transforming the red of blood to royal purple. You could decide on a color that represents the person you are now. You could also choose a moonstone to symbolize your enduring spiritual connection with the moon, whose cycles will continue to govern your biorhythms on a more subtle level.

AGES 51 TO 60

The Age of Sovereignty

WE'VE HAD OUR GOLDEN BIRTHDAY and we're in our fifties now. This is the age of sovereignty, but that doesn't necessarily mean it will be easy. At the beginning of this decade many women will be finishing menopause, with all its swings and surprises, and no sooner is that over than Saturn rolls in, and we're plunged into the transformative chaos of the second Saturn Return. All in all, we're likely to be dealing with a time of transition reminiscent of the chaos of adolescence. This time, though, we have half a century of experience to help us take charge of our lives and get through.

Many are disconcerted to find themselves, at fifty-one, eligible to join the American Association of Retired People and feel rather guilty if they take advantage of its benefits. Surely that's for *old* people—we're only, well, "middle-aged." In fact, these days, that's quite true. As life expectancy edges toward the century mark, a fifty-year-old may well be at the midpoint of life. Just as adolescence is a time of transition that prepares the child to live in the adult world, the fifties may be seen as a time during which we will begin to think about our "second adulthood" and acquire the information and skills we'll need to survive it.

During this decade, some people will in fact retire from their first career and start a second, perhaps going back to college for retraining or for the degree they never finished the first time around. Susan B. Anthony and Elizabeth Cady Stanton, who originally met when they were in their thirties while supporting the cause of Temperance, realized that equal rights for women were a greater priority, and in their fifties founded the National Women's Suffrage Association. In *The Second Stage,* Betty Friedan critiqued the myth of the feminist mystique that had been partially created by her earlier work.

Others are delighted to find themselves becoming grandparents. They may even become parents once more, if they end up having to take over and raise their grandchildren. For others, intergenerational caregiving goes in the other direction, as they find it necessary to give an aging parent a home. In a worst-case scenario they may be caught in the middle, with obligations in both directions.

This may also be a time when we feel the first touch of mortality. We hear of friends our own age who have sudden heart attacks. Parents may leave us at any time from now on. Death is changing from a stranger to an acquaintance who we hope will wait a long time to become a friend.

On the other hand, the fifties can provide an optimal balance of energy and experience, the crown of life, when we are old enough both to know what we want and how to get it. Now is the time to come to grips with life and make it give us what we need.

		FATE DATES FOR AGES 51 TO 60	

Ages 42–55	♄ □ ♄	Saturn squares self	•Prime time begins! •"In between" stage can be confusing •Possible depression, intimations of mortality •Questions about future
Ages 50–52	⚷	Chiron returns	•Heal inner wounds
Ages 55–57	♄ ⚹ ♄	Saturn sextiles self	•Major turning point
	♅ △ ♅	Uranus trines self	•Life direction changes
	♆ △ ♆	Neptune trines self	•New desires, focus •Life more creative, less stress •Men's feelings more available •Women more independent •More community activity or new work, career, or school •Spiritual quest, release illusions •No more need to live up to expectations
	☊☋	Moon nodes return	•Time for self-examination
Ages 56–60	♄ ☌ ♄	Saturn returns	•Time to "let go"
Ages 59–61	♅ □ ♅	Uranus squares self	•Challenge or complacency? •Time to review history, find undeveloped creativity •Explore personal philosophy, freedom, awareness •Re-evaluate commitments, create opportunities for enrichment •Awareness of age and aging
Age 60	♃ ☌ ♃	Jupiter returns	•Identity develops

Fifty-one

B ETWEEN AGE FIFTY AND FIFTY-TWO the asteroid Chiron will be returning to his natal position in your chart. In mythology, he is the wounded healer, you may find that this is a painful time for you as well. The wound can be outer—an accident, psychological or emotional—or inner—the loss of a parent. Which one you receive will depend on your personal destiny. Hang in there—the wound will heal eventually, and if you make use of the pain, leave you wiser.

But don't go looking for trouble. As Z puts it, "I don't buy the idea that you have to suffer in order to become a better person, but life is old-fashioned, and the Fates dish it out on the dime. So no bungee jumping, or pushing the envelope. The Fates will take you down if you tempt them!"

It's a time for opening up, as well as for re-evaluation, as Diana discovered at her thirtieth college reunion:

> Both my old roommates were there, and we had a grand time catching up. I always find this pentannual opportunity to check in with women of my own age group interesting. It seems to me that as we grow older, our shared experience at Mills has given us a unique perspective. This time, especially, I found myself making a real contact with women with whom I thought I had nothing in common when we were at school. We all seem to be going through a menopausal reassessment, and everyone was much more willing to open up and actually communicate.

THE BIRTHDAY

If you try to put fifty-one candles on the cake you'll have too many to light, so try representing the decades with larger red candles, and the years with smaller white ones. Five is the number of change, and one is for the direction you are going. Can you see where it leads?

Fifty-two

A T THE BEGINNING OF YOUR FIFTIES, Saturn squares his own natal point in your life, sits down for a while, and has tea, letting you catch your breath before the next cycle of change begins. The years between fifty-two and fifty-nine, like those between twenty-two and twenty-nine, can be a time of new responsibilities and great productivity. And yet, as the Roman version of the Greek Chronos, the deity of Time, he inevitably brings with him an awareness of mortality, often as the result of some health issue that becomes a problem at this time.

We're all subject to it, and we all try to avoid facing it. The kind of death-by-violence that we have become accustomed to in the media provides excitement, not understanding. It is rare for someone to die of old age in the movies, even though that is how a majority of us will pass. So we become Crones in denial, unwilling to consider that death may only be life in another form. When parents die, we are forced to face our own mortality. For Diana, this was a time of transition, when her mother-in-law, who had shared her home from the beginning of Diana's marriage, passed away. In the same year, her first grandson was born, and she herself became the family matriarch.

It is a good thing that Saturn is taking his time, and giving us time to get used to the idea. Take this opportunity for contemplation. If you ever want to understand what something means to you, imagine it gone. Suddenly you'll have a better appreciation of what it, or he, or she, is doing in your life. Death gives meaning to both people and things—death, and time, which in some respects are the same.

So what if your body is aging? Your soul is immortal. But your body has been your faithful partner all these years. Be kind to her, have patience with her aches and pains. Don't let depression get you down. If your cat or dog were ailing, you would research treatments and cures. Do the same for your body.

Cass observes that she feels "a little creaky when the weather changes. Otherwise, wonderful. I'm in my Cronehood! Yay! I've learned to acknowledge the dark places in me. I have changed many old patterns of living."

Vandimir says, "It feels good when people think I may be old enough to have something to say. It feels sad when people think I'm just an old dinosaur. It feels good to be able to rely on memories and past experiences to get through new challenges. It feels bad when my body tells me I can't do all the things I used to."

The developing awareness of this age makes it a good time for working on your spiritual life. It matters little by what name you call on the Divine, or what sacred books you read, as long as you don't get sucked in by those religions that want to convert the world to their particular brand of religious mind-spin. They offer not nourishment, but poison. Just now you are very sensitive to spiritual influences, so be careful, and follow the path that gives you comfort.

THE BIRTHDAY

Rather than putting the five candles for the decades and two for the years on your cake, set them on a plate or tray in the center of the table. Select candles in the appropriate colors and use them to bless your chakras, the seven energy centers in the body as described in Hindu tradition.

Light the red candle and say, "I light this candle to bless my body and my connection to the Earth...."

Light the orange candle and say, "I light this candle to bless my sexuality...."

Light the yellow candle and say, "I light this candle to bless my center of power...."

Light the green candle and say, "I light this candle to bless my power to love...."

Light the bright blue candle and say, "I light this candle to bless my words...."

Light the dark blue candle and say, "I light this candle to bless my inner vision...."

Light the purple candle and say, "I light this candle to connect me to Spirit...."

Let them burn throughout your birthday dinner, and keep them to light when you need to energize one or another of your chakras throughout the coming year.

Fifty-three

NOW, TIME SEEMS TO BE SLOWING DOWN. You are moving into the fullness of your sovereignty, with the power to put a final polish on your Second Destiny. Look both back and forward—you have work to do.

If you have prospered, begin to pay forward by sharing your talents with others. Since you were young, the world has changed. The new generation is looking for help, advice, approval. Volunteer your time and skills to teach those who will follow. On the other hand, perhaps you are still deeply involved in your second mission. You have the rest of this decade to get it all together—don't waste these precious years striving for security. Fear less, and love more. Follow your heart. This is a good time to take that trip you've dreamed of, while you have both the experience to appreciate it and the energy to do it.

The Fates don't micromanage—don't look to them for instructions concerning the small picture. They have created the generational context—your job is to make good choices that will put you in harmony with this larger plan. If you want to know more about how to do this, work with a divination system such as tarot. A good tarot reader or astrologer will be able to help you interpret the symbols. You can use a pendulum yourself to get "Yes/No" answers. Divination enables you to get the left and right brain talking to each other. Your deep self has a lot of useful wisdom if you can learn how to hear what it has to say.

Now is a good time to review your personal destiny. The universe is giving you a three-year free period before Saturn comes back to kick you into more change. So allow yourself to mature, like a fine wine....

Rachael says that for her fifty-third birthday her friends threw her a five-day party. Of her feelings about being this age, she states, "I feel it in every joint I own, but it's not nearly so bad as the alternative. I finally understand my grandmother. I find that I am much more tolerant than those who are younger than I am. I also find that I am more patient and a lot more willing to let the world make its mistakes and to give it time to correct them."

For Diana, this year brought a deeper involvement in the heathen section of the pagan community. "I was awarded the title of Elder and elected to the Board of Directors of the Troth, just in time to use my experience with nonprofit religious organizations to help it survive a major reorganization. I realized that I had both the knowledge and patience to ride the storm. At this point in my life, the concept 'This too shall pass' has a lot more meaning for me than it does for the younger crew."

THE BIRTHDAY

Take this opportunity for some R&R—"Rest and Reflection." Take a trip by yourself to some nice bed-and-breakfast place where you can walk or sit and admire the view. Celebrate your birthday like a season, savoring the process of change. Schedule dinner with friends, not all together, but individually. Take the opportunity for some one-on-one soul sharing.

Fifty-four

A STROLOGICALLY, THIS IS ANOTHER PEACEFUL YEAR for those of your generation. You should check out your own chart, however, for developments that may affect you alone. Be aware, also, that those who are a bit ahead of you in age are beginning to go through some changes.

Brianna comments that at this age,

> *my knees hurt. I've been getting wiser and deeper. There's a shift and a darkening that comes when you begin to age, and begin to have people around you aging, ailing, and dying. In former times, I suppose, this was the common human condition, but in our*

lifetimes it's been possible to reach middle age without having to focus on it. In my fifties I've been confronted with the needs of frail elders who are close to me, with the illness and death of some of my own contemporaries, the premature deaths of children I helped to raise.

Even if you yourself are still healthy and strong, you know that these others are showing you the road ahead. At the same time, I enjoy life with a depth and intensity that I never did before; because I am pretty constantly aware that it is a precious, finite thing, and because I'm coming to understand my own priorities so much more clearly....

As you grow older, you develop the understanding that different ages really are stages that we all pass through—when you are younger you may know this on an intellectual level, but on a gut level you really don't get it. You somehow feel as though people of different ages are intrinsically different kinds of people, so that getting older gives you the last laugh—you know that young people will be your age some day, but they don't know that yet.

In the middle fifties, the results of life choices about health care and exercise begin to become apparent. Now is the time when those with a genetic tendency to blood sugar problems may develop adult onset diabetes. For many, the disease can be controlled by paying attention to your diet and starting an exercise program.

This is also a time when those with the potential for heart trouble, especially men, may have sudden, devastating heart attacks. If you have a male partner who smokes, or does not eat well or exercise, insist that he have a complete checkup, including testing for blood cholesterol. Men who can make it through their fifties have a good chance at a healthy old age, but their mates and families may have to do some work to get them there.

THE BIRTHDAY

Take this opportunity to pay attention to your body, too. Have you been putting off getting a health checkup? Schedule one today, including a mammogram. Pamper yourself with a massage, or take a friend and visit a hot tub.

Living in a body is part of being in the world. Pack an elegant little lunch and go for a picnic somewhere you can sit on the ground and feel the Earth energies, feel the sun on your back and listen to the wind whispering in the trees. Every season has its beauties, including your own. . . .

Fifty-five

IT'S MID-DECADE—YOU HAVE ONE MORE YEAR to go before Saturn rolls back into your life. Make the most of it. If enjoyment of life is an indicator of success, you can make yourself successful by brushing up your social skills. Get off that couch and go dancing while you still can!

Even though Saturn hasn't quite got here yet, the other planets are moving. Uranus, the great Quick Changer, and Neptune, Ruler of Imagination, are both moving to trine their natal point. They provide the energy for new insights, and the third return of your moon nodes to their natal point provides the diesel fuel for change. A similar movement occurred when you were forty-four to forty-five. Now you are turning again.

It starts with a keen desire for something different, something better. Uranus is not a gentle visitor; his influence is seductive and makes the heart leap. Neptune creates for us a new paradigm. Looking through this new lens we can imagine ourselves anew.

When Neptune trines itself, it can introduce a new spiritual quest and release us from some illusions. We begin to realize that we no longer have to live up to the expectations of others, particularly those others who dominated our lives when we were younger. We're beginning to glimpse a new goal, to become who and what we ourselves want to be, even if it's against all logic! This is the train we have to catch to improve our lives and fulfill our full potential.

Gabriele from Germany writes:

> *Only during the last years have I started feeling, experiencing*
> *myself. During my younger years I was pretty "dumb"; I didn't*
> *feel myself, I didn't feel other people. Somehow I sometimes think*
> *it was as if I hadn't really been there. Now I am getting to know*
> *(pretty slowly) that there are other dimensions in life than the*
> *"real world" and I am trying to learn. I would never want to be*
> *young again. I do appreciate the knowledge (I don't know that*
> *"knowledge" is the right word—it is more like "wisdom" but this*
> *is too big a word, isn't it?) I have now. I can see and feel lots of*
> *things in different ways, healthier ways, and even in my job (I*
> *teach 12-16-year-olds) I keep learning and organizing things in*
> *new ways.*
>
> *It is like a big permanent adventure, and as I said above, I*
> *wouldn't want to go back. Having all those experiences is a*
> *treasure. On the other hand, my body seems to become more deli-*
> *cate, pains every now and then, lots of little things that hurt or*
> *make things more difficult, but I can forget about these most of*
> *the time. . . . I have less strength and am becoming physically*
> *weaker, but mental power seems to be growing.*

THE BIRTHDAY

It's spiritual renewal time again! You're fifty-five—a double pentagram.
The five points of the pentagram (from upper right clockwise around)
represent Air, Earth, Water, Fire, and Spirit. Take a good hard look at
your life and decide what needs to be fixed or improved.

The first point, Air, relates to communication. Is there someone
important from whom you're estranged because of miscommunica-
tion, or someone you simply haven't gotten in touch with for far too
long? Pick up the phone or write a letter today.

Second, look at Earth, your support and foundation. Contemplating
this area can point you toward necessary repairs to the home you live
in, but for most of us, it means looking at our finances. Do you know

what your financial situation is? Do you have a budget? A retirement plan?

Third, consider Water, which governs our emotions. Who do you love? What makes you happy? Put some fun in your life. Make plans to spend some time with people whose company you really enjoy, doing things that will lift your spirits.

Fourth, pay attention to Fire, the fuel that keeps us going. Now is the time to zero in on the passion that really impels you. When do you feel most excited and alive? Fire's energy may be neither comfortable nor comforting, but it will give you a goal.

The fifth point brings you back to Spirit. With all the energy released by your work with the four elements, don't forget to take some time to look inward and open up to the power of the spirit, whether it takes on the form of dancing around the fire with other women to honor the Goddess or sitting in meditation in a church or a Japanese garden.

Put two sets of five candles in a pentagram pattern on a plate or on your birthday cake. As you light the outermost, name the element that it represents. Then light its inner partner and state what you have done to bring its influence into your life, or what you plan to do.

Fifty-six

ALL RIGHT EVERYBODY—IT'S TIME TO STOP COASTING! Tremendous forces have been set in motion; the Fates are stirring the great universal cauldron with both hands. Twenty-eight years have passed since Saturn returned to his natal position the first time, and now he's on his way back for another round, looking to see if you did the homework he set you last time. Hope you have rested up, because from now on inner and outer transformations will be happening on several levels. You're moving into another long-lasting period of change. The influence of Uranus and Neptune will continue to make you restless.

Diana celebrated the official beginning of her second Saturn Return by moving into the attic:

To understand this, you have to realize that we have a very big house, which has always been home to a lot of people. I now share it with my son, daughter-in-law, and three grandchildren. The attic is a multi-level space which was remodeled as an apartment for my mother-in-law, who lived with us from my marriage until she died when I was fifty-one.

Now I am the grandmother, and I realized that I would have a lot more peace of mind, not to mention privacy, if I was not trying to sleep and work on the same floor with my three grandchildren. So I volunteered to move into my mother-in-law's old space and give up my room to the kids.

Moving out of a room in which you have lived for almost thirty years requires major excavation. As I dug through the strata I felt as if I was reliving my Second Destiny. It was painful to decide what to give away, what to throw away, and what I had to somehow find room for upstairs. In claiming this new space, I felt as if I were redefining myself.

Z also found herself wanting something new:

I was overcome with the uncontrollable desire to write screenplays. I took off three years from writing books and wrote three screenplays. I'd like to do two more movies and a sitcom. I think the last one was rather good, but unfortunately in Hollywood a writer without an agent has a snowball's chance in hell. Still, I've got a lot of moxie, and I wanted to try. Instinct assures me that if I make myself a player, the Fates will favor me. It hasn't happened yet, and I've gone back to writing books like this one, but one of these days I'll find the right agent....

THE BIRTHDAY

Welcome Saturn into your life—if you don't try to hold him at arm's length maybe he'll go easy on you this year! Offer him a toast before you blow out your birthday candles. Thank him for the energy that carried you through your second mission, and as you look at those glowing candles, take some time to think about the gains and losses, the lessons and achievements, they represent. Say a few words about the things you've done during the past twenty-eight years. Say farewell to your Second Destiny.

Fifty-seven

THIS IS LIKELY TO BE A CHALLENGING YEAR. The third moon node return is still in place, opening windows of insight into our mission in life. Since we have just finished our second mission, now is the time to seek for a glimpse of the third. This nodal cycle marks the return of inspiration and spiritual awareness. Use this opportunity for self-examination and the review of spiritual commitments. If this provokes a "dark night of the soul," don't give up hope. It's all part of the learning process.

In addition, Saturn is in the middle of his return, and it will be a year or two before he has completed the cycle. So this year, we are in the midst of being rebuilt and redesigned, like a half-sewn dress with the bottom and maybe the sleeves still missing. No wonder we get depressed.

Z comments that when she goes walking in the cemetery with her dogs she checks the ages on the tombstones. Fifty-seven is one of those years when a lot of people seem to die. Why? Because people think that ending a big mission like the one that goes with our Second Destiny is a tragedy. They don't consider that life has to close down old eras in order to open up new ones.

People who have paid little attention to spiritual matters seem to suffer the most. The mind must be rooted in spirit. If the spirit is not acknowledged, the mind will have to find some other way to tap in to the energy of the universe, and that's not easy. Mental and spiritual health are connected, so this is a time to learn the techniques of meditation and calm the chattering mind, or to strengthen the spirit through ritual. Daily prayer or meditation are ways to give love to ourselves—

they will nourish the soul. Much the same effect can come from reading inspiring or sacred poetry.

But we must also pay attention to our bodies. A good diet will help fight depression. Lecithin and soy products soothe the nerves. St. John's Wort is a mood elevator that has been used for centuries. Despite television propaganda, the pharmaceutical industry is not the only source of help. This is a good time to do some research into health. If you are taking herbs, get a good book that will teach you about dosage and interactions. If you are taking drugs, get a book that covers their side effects. Work on those things you have some power over—your body and how you take care of it. The internal spiritual rearrangement will occur on its own.

Victoria has some comments:

> *My age feels like the closing of many doors, and the opening of others. At fifty-seven, I know that I am no longer in a desirable demographic, and no, I am not talking about sexuality here. I become more prudent, consume less, and am not so likely to be seduced by the promises that this brand of detergent or that shade of lipstick will enhance my quality of life. . . . I am no longer in the age group that television and print advertisers covet because I am now invulnerable to their blandishments. That Yankee adage of "Wear it out, use it up, make do" seems now to be my approach to material things. I don't want or need the newest of the new.*
>
> *In the work world, I find my age, maturity, judgment, and discernment are valued if I am already present at the table, but the problem is getting invited. Companies in the Bay Area promise would-be recruits that "here you won't have to work for your mother," and I am at an age at which I look and feel like everyone's mother.*

THE BIRTHDAY

The energy for this year is going to be challenging, so your presents for this birthday should help you to prepare for it. Tell your friends that the gifts you want include books on herbs, nutrition, inspirational writings, some money toward that workshop you've been wanting to take. Schedule a medical checkup so you know what you've got to work with. And then, for the birthday itself, do something totally entertaining or silly! Go to a show, wear funny party hats, blow up balloons, and get your friends to play games. Rev up those endorphins—you'll need them!

Fifty-eight

IT'S TIME TO TREAD LIGHTLY. Saturn is still moving through our charts, so we had better not look for big changes in our lives anytime soon. This is a waiting period. The check is in the mail. . . . We need to spend this year getting ready for the next mission, whatever it turns out to be. We can take care of our health and change our habits. This is a good time to take up a new study, learn a new language or skill.

It's also a time for soul-searching. If we have made bad choices earlier, the results all come home to roost now. We need to try to understand what has happened and why, to admit and understand our own problems, and take steps to solve them. All this can lead to a loss of spirit and purpose. Forced retirement or an empty nest can cause depression. We feel we've been rejected, and forget that our failures, as well as our successes, were part of the Second Destiny.

At this point in our lives we need the support of a group of friends in the same situation or some kind of therapy. To have someone listen to our problems and supply a sane point of view helps us sort things out. A good therapist is nonjudgmental. She helps us to question ourselves and answer our own questions. Therapy can provide us with a qualified coach as we work on ourselves.

We have to remember—surviving the Saturn Return is proof that the soul can be reborn. Saturn's cycle provides the structure for our personal histories. We need to pay attention to his lessons.

Diana comments on the turmoil of the second Saturn Return:

In hindsight, the shifts of my first Saturn Return were so obvious that I thought the second one would be easy to understand when it came along. But I was still in the midst of its turmoil. For the first time since I sold my first book, a novel proposal was rejected, and I was wondering whether I still had a career as a fiction writer. There were more novels that I wanted to write; on the other hand, I felt a building pressure to harvest the fruits of thirty years as a priestess and get them out into the world. But the way to achieve that goal was not yet clear. I also felt a need to reclaim the ability to paint that I abandoned years ago. Going through my Saturn Return at the same time that the world was shifting from one millennium to another has been . . . interesting. It's clear that a significant chapter in my life has ended, but where the road leads now I do not know. . . .

DeeAnne comments:

I am somewhat sad that I still have not done something spectacular with my life. I haven't achieved any kind of status or fame. I haven't mastered any particular skill. I am not rich . . . nor have I reached any pinnacle in a career. I am still plodding along as I always have, trying to keep a roof over my head, food in my belly. I do believe I have more experience from which to draw when making a decision or when asked for advice. It is reassuring to know this. I have learned to trust in the universe and to know that my life unfolds exactly the way it should.

I have suffered from the loss of friendship, even from intentional harm inflicted by those whom I once loved. I have worked through the anger inside . . . and have been able to reach a place of peace and forgiveness . . . and as a result, find release. I have known what it is to lose family, having lost my parents while still a young adult and my only sibling far too early in life. I have learned to be independent, having been alone most of my adult life. I have learned the joys of motherhood, raising three children, and have been able to share in their parenthood by having the love of five beautiful children who call me Nana.

I think the greatest gift of all in my advancing years is having the opportunity to love again. For it is in this year of being fifty-eight that I have found love. With the heart of an adventurer, I flew off a comfortable and secure cliff into the unknown realm of "relationship." Since it has been almost twenty-four years since I seriously attempted one, it has been quite an experience, but a risk well worth all that I sacrificed. To leave family, remove almost all material possessions holding me to "place," I have become once more a free spirit swept away by the wind, returning to the land of my birth, acting on one of life's most precious gifts, to begin a new life. Having risked all, I will grow old, secure in my love of another and of being loved in return. . . .

There is not much that life has not put in front of me to experience, and through it all, I have always found life to be a wonder! This thing we do, in living, is beautiful, even when you are about to turn fifty-nine!

THE BIRTHDAY

Comfort. This year, that's what you need. Celebrate your birthday in comfortable clothes, with comfortable food, and comfortable friends. Life will challenge you enough this year. Take this opportunity to have a simple, undemanding party. Make it a potluck, to which everyone brings her favorite comfort food. So what if it's all dessert? Indulge yourself! Rent a well-loved movie and lounge about together to watch it (cheerful is best, unless you really enjoy having a good cry). Think up something really interesting and fun you would like to do or learn in the coming year.

Fifty-nine

THIS YEAR THE WHEELS OF FORTUNE will turn once more, carrying Saturn away. It's still a challenging time, but the planets are brewing you some changes. Saturn is on his way out, but Uranus the great Changer is squaring his natal point, a position he will hold until we are sixty-one. Once more, we need to get rid of the psychic baggage we've been carrying with us so that we can get on with our lives. Uranus helps us in this endeavor by opening up our perceptions. Sometimes this brings us a new perspective on religion. We may take a more active interest in our church or investigate a new form of spirituality.

Uranus always brings something unexpected. When he is squared, the conflict increases. His role in our lives this year will be to help us "let go," which is crucial when we are between destinies. Uranus governs the ongoing process by which we release aspects of the personality that are no longer needed and allow new ones to emerge. The third planet, Jupiter, will move into our lives toward the end of the year, lulling us to complacency, or pushing us to greater achievement. Which will we choose? Whatever we do, this year will give us a chance to review our lives and bring to light undeveloped creative activities. Between Saturn and Uranus, at age fifty-nine, we are like a wine in which the yeast is still working. The fermentation of character will cause us to mature and gain peace of mind—eventually.

This birthday has been especially significant to Diana, because it occurred when she was putting the finishing touches on this book:

> *Where last year I was still in the midst of Saturn's turmoil, as of this moment, I'm beginning to see light at the end of the tunnel. The weather is chilly, but I find my spirits lifting. For one thing, writing this book has helped me to put my own life experiences into perspective. I am truly grateful to all those who responded to our plea and sent in their stories. I am hoping that this book will be the first of many in which I can share what I have learned. I'm teaching a new class that is being well received. Furthermore, a long-awaited novel contract is in the mail, so there's hope on that front as well. Now if I can just get my bones to stay put and get back to regular exercise, life will be beautiful!*

THE BIRTHDAY

Whatever else may have been planned for you by family or friends, have a private little ceremony of your own on your birthday at dawn.

If you are not a morning person, this may not seem like such a wonderful idea, but make the effort. The harder it is to get out of bed, the more benefit in doing so. You are at the dawn of your Third Destiny, and it will be beautiful, but you will still have to work to make it happen.

So find out when the sun is going to come up, and set your alarm. Set up a little table in the East—if possible in front of a window—with a candle, a small cake, and a glass and a small bottle of sparkling water or champagne. Use a frosting tube to inscribe the ancient rune for the dawning— ᛉ —on the cake. It looks something like an angular eternity symbol, or like a stylized butterfly.

When you wake up, go to your birthday table. Light the candle, and if you are in front of a window, open the curtain. Pour a glass of bubbly and raise it in toast to the rising sun. Say something like:

> *Hail to you, Mother Sun!*
> *A blessing on the new day you bring!*
> *Bless also the new year you are bringing me—*
> *New life, new love, a rebirth of the spirit.*
> *Let your radiant light shine brightly*
> *And reveal my Third Destiny....*

Then drink the bubbly and eat the cake. (NOTE: In northern Europe, the sun was always feminine.)

Sixty

CONGRATULATIONS—YOU'VE MADE IT through your second Saturn Return. Jupiter is back, bringing you new ambition and energy. You are off the hinge, and are beginning to internalize and integrate the lessons you learned. Now it's time to pay attention to your body! Sixty is a watershed year. Many people don't make it this far. The early sixties will be a dangerous period for those with weak constitutions, so if you want that Third Destiny, be careful!

The starwork for this age is the fight against depression, because it lurks in the background whenever we confront our mortality. Depression can be one effect of the Saturn Return, but it's not a disease, it's a transition, and so it will pass. If you are dissatisfied with what you've done in your life, now's the time to change it.

Take this opportunity to re-evaluate your personal philosophy and open up your awareness. It's a tall order. The commitments we've already made can intensify and increase in importance. Consider them carefully—which of these things do you really *need* to do? We need to get our priorities clear in order to make changes. If we create the time and opportunity to work on the issues that really matter, we can continue to be enriched and reach out to our communities.

THE BIRTHDAY

Dana writes, "It was my sixtieth that was the one, the Year of the Metal Dragon, and my return to my birth sign and element. On my birthday I was destroyed and built anew with runes of power by the sisters and brothers of my circle. The next day I received my Ph.D. at the Graduate Theological Union, my dissertation work having been on folk elements of Mary legends and in the fields of History of Religions and Folklore."

Not everyone has such notable passages with which to mark this birthday, but reaching the age of sixty is certainly reason enough for a major celebration. Invite friends from every decade of your life. Dig out your photo albums and mount a display. If you feel funny about doing all this for yourself, hand all the material over to a friend or one of your children to organize.

Worried about letting people know that you're this old? Rub their noses in it! Sixty isn't what it used to be. You've got twenty or more good years left in you and you're revving up for your Third Destiny—let the rest of the world be warned!

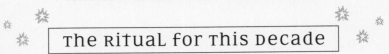

The Ritual for This Decade

THE HINGE OF FATE: A PASSAGE FOR THE SECOND SATURN RETURN

If our first Saturn Return was difficult because it was so unexpected, because we felt we had barely got the hang of our first mission before it changed, the second can be hard because we have been entrenched in our second mission for almost thirty years. The hinges of our spirits may be as creaky as our joints are getting. Knowing that change is necessary and inevitable doesn't make it any easier to give up old habits and assumptions. We come to this passage full of anxieties, about health, relationships, and jobs.

The hectic evolutionary pace of the twentieth century seems likely to continue into the twenty-first. The one thing we know for sure is that the world is not going to stay the same. And neither, of course, will we. The door of fate is opening, but what is on the other side? Will the Third Destiny be as productive as the second one, or are we going to dwindle sadly into old age? From now on, the differences between those who say "Yes" to destiny and those who retreat from it will become more and more obvious.

Through ritual, we internalize wisdom that may not be accepted by the conscious mind. Through this rite of passage we can send our souls the message that we want a positive Third Destiny. This ritual can be performed at any time after the fifty-sixth birthday, when you feel that the unsettling energy of Saturn's return has stirred up your unconscious sufficiently for it to be helpful.

PREPARATION

The ritual will be more meaningful if you put some time and energy into preparation. If possible, take a weekend at some point in the month before the ritual for a retreat. Go off by yourself somewhere quiet, preferably in the countryside where there are places you can walk in the woods or gaze out at the sea. For the first day, don't try to do anything but let yourself relax. On the second, get out a notepad and tear off two pieces of paper. One is headed, "Things I want to get rid of"; the other, "Things I want in my future."

Take some time to contemplate your life. What do you value? What do you really need? As each element comes to mind, imagine what would happen if it were to disappear. Look at jobs, hobbies, possessions, relationships, health—make no exceptions. Write down the things that are cluttering your life without contributing to its quality. The Norn who rules the Third Destiny is called Skuld. One meaning of her name is "debt"—that which must be paid or fulfilled. So when you have finished listing things you want to get rid of, list any debts, financial or personal, that you may owe, and draw up a plan to deal with them.

When you have done that, put down the paper and do something active that will get the blood circulating. After your break, take up the second piece of paper. Try to imagine yourself in ten years, or in twenty. What would you like to be doing? How do you see yourself then? What things need to happen in order for those outcomes to occur? Some of the things you want are already in your life. Some will be new. Take your list of debts and make plans to pay them. If you have wronged anyone, look for some means of restitution. If that is impossible, look for a way to "pay forward" by helping someone else.

Bring the lists you have made during the weekend retreat with you to the ritual.

THE RITUAL

Immediately before the rite, you should take a purifying bath. If you desire, you may do a modified fast (fruit juice and tea) as well, so that you will be clean in body as well as spirit.

Decorate the ritual room in black and silver with the astrological symbol for Saturn on a banner. Put the food in a second, adjoining room for the celebration. This is a good party to which to invite a variety of people whom you have known in various contexts over the years.

If several women are going through their Saturn Return at the same time, you may celebrate the passage together. Set up altars on each side of the room, one draped in red, with a lit red candle and metal baking tray on it, and the other draped in black, with an unlit silver candle. You should have with you the list of things you are giving up, tied with a red ribbon, and your list of hopes for the future, tied in silver.

You (and your companions) enter and stand in the middle, between them. Go to the red altar, which represents the past, and hold out the list you made of things you no longer need. Explain to the group what it is, and if you feel comfortable doing so, read all or some of it. When you have done so, say that you are releasing these things, light the paper, and set it on the tray to burn. If there are several of you, each one does the same in turn. Then blow out the candle.

You have now left your past, which was ruled first by the Norn called Urdh (that which has been) and then by her sister Verdandi (that which is becoming), behind you. Now it is time to pass through the swinging door of fate into the power of Skuld—that which *shall* be.

Everyone sings the following chant, which came out of the work done by the senior Queen group at the Goddess 2000 festival.

I am the hinge of fate, and I am opening the door

and I am changing you are changing me....

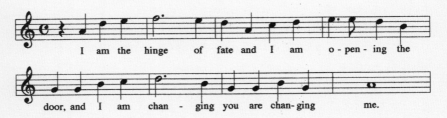

When the energy is flowing well, begin to move. If you are the only initiate, twirl in place, or invite an older friend to link right arms with you and begin to spin. If there are several making the passage, you can divide into even numbers and swing each other. Get some speed up—you want to really *feel* the energy that is swinging you around.

When you can hold on no longer, let the momentum spin you toward the black draped altar. When you have caught your breath, bow before it (bowing your head will be sufficient if your knees are not up to kneeling!).

Each one making the passage asks permission to enter the Third Destiny, and offers her list of hopes and plans. Say, "I wish that what should be, shall be!"

Then go forth through the door into the room that has been prepared for the celebration, and begin your Third Destiny.

AGES 61 TO 70

Older or Elder?

SIXTY YEARS AND COUNTING ... the Age of Gold becomes the Diamond Jubilee. But we find ourselves asking whether this a time for anxiety or celebration. Because the average life expectancy is being so dramatically extended, those who move into their sixties in the twenty-first century have the potential to experience these years in a way unknown to any previous generation. Soon, there will be more people in the United States who are over sixty-five than who are under fifteen, and they will live to their eighties or longer. Despite current worries about Social Security, it still gives more seniors a better safety net than we have ever had before.

Questions abound. Are we growing old or are we entering our second adulthood? For many, completion of the second Saturn Return creates a sense of closure. The careers that have utilized all our energies for the past thirty years may no longer satisfy us. Changing job markets may make us redundant. Is it time to retire or to seek a different way of making a living? What do we want to do now that we are reaching full maturity? Will we have the resources, both physical and economic, to do it?

The Third Destiny starts with a challenge—we must decide whether to accept it or to give up hope and break down. It is essential to find a new mission and go for it, otherwise we'll feel useless. We no longer need the approval of others. We don't have to compete. The projects we choose now are the things *we* feel need to be done to make the world better. Look at it this way—if we are busy, we won't have so much time to count our aches and pains.

We can contemplate the prospect of living for thirty or forty more years as a gift or a penalty. We are pathfinders in a new territory, and our response to this challenge may well determine not only the way in which we live our own lives, but the experience of many who come after us.

The sixth decade can bring many surprises. Morganna, who at sixty-four is happily living with a lover twenty-five years younger, sent us this lovely poem:

YESTERDAY

I thought my life was full
there was nothing more that I needed
I rushed through hours, days and weeks
and for years I succeeded
in managing to bury quite deeply
a part of me that never heeded
or acknowledged what I would feel when I met you!

TODAY

I know that my life is full
and I have what my heart requires
to live in joy and happiness
and to realize all of my desires
You have brought completeness to me
you have made me feel authentic
you have given me more joy than I've believed possible

and my heart feels more love
than I can possibly express.

TOMORROW

I refuse to look beyond next week, next month
I have no idea what the future holds in store
I can only walk one day at a time
Not daring to wish for anything more.

So for now—
I'm gonna dance like no one is watching
I'm gonna love without fearing a broken heart
because if I didn't take this chance
I might have spared myself some pain, but—
I would have missed the dance.

FATE DATES FOR AGES 61 TO 70

Ages 61-65   ♄ ☌ ♄   Saturn return ending   •Rite of passage to maturity

♅ □ ♅   Uranus squares self   •New sense of direction
•Liberation or death
•New interests, studies
•Rush of inspiration

Ages 65-67   ♄ □ ♄   Saturn squares self   •Change self-image to Elderhood, wisdom
•Grieve for lost youth and accept age
•Choose to give up or keep going
•Identify real priorities

Sixty-one

A T SIXTY-ONE WE HAVE STARTED A NEW DECADE, but the fermentation of character and worldview that started with the second Saturn Return is still going on. It's time to finally let go of the Second Destiny. It's finished—we need to make room for the new mission that's coming in. This year Uranus will be squaring his natal point, and we feel restless, we are getting new ideas and are uncomfortable standing still. This is a time to review leftover rebellions. Give them some action both from within and without. Submerge yourself in the holiness of life and relentlessly pursue liberation.

It's time to shed the old stuff. Clean out your closets, and if you haven't worn a garment for three years, give it away. Go through your books as well. If it's not something you reread for comfort or use for reference why is it still on your shelves? Find a used bookstore or library that will get those books to the people who need them now. Scrape the past off your back as a whale scrapes off barnacles. You'll swim much more freely.

Every time we complete a passage, we think, "Okay, I'm done—I'm grown up now!" And then we come to a new threshold and it all changes again. This time, the new challenge is to become a wisewoman. It will take awhile. To do this work we will have to focus on ourselves once more. But by now, family and social responsibilities are decreasing. The responsibilities we still carry are those that we have chosen, a part of our spiritual path.

The beginning of the sixth decade is a good time to look back and take stock. Dana writes:

> I'm sixty-one, going on sixteen, going on a hundred and fourteen. A few weeks ago I was an officiating priestess at Twilight Gathering, representing the mystery of Birth on a gravel bar island in a river in the redwoods, and I was all the power and knowledge of the Midwife, in her warrior strength of wise one. The integration has begun. Being a Crone is not being old and

debilitated. It is being whole, drawing on the power of each phase of life, and completing it with all the other phases that have passed sequentially by. Now I have the mystery in hand and heart and mind. I am a web, a spider web of being and memory. Now I am a matrix, and all I see and do is in patterns, not lines. . . .

When I turned sixty, I collected the long overdue initiations, my Ph.D. hood, and two elevations to Elder in the Craft. And I found that my heart's desire lies with sitting with my cats and learning the great magic that they are born with. And taking that magic with me into the world, a different kind of urban shaman. And I have gathered up the threads of the Virgin Maiden, the Queen of Desire, the Great Mother, the Amazon Warrior, the Wise Woman, and the Crone, although perhaps She is yet to come. And I look down what I hope is still a long road to see what I can do and be for the next decades.

How the world has changed! From the simplistic patriotism of the forties, to the oppression of the fifties, the short burst of freedom of the sixties and seventies, to the commercialism of the eighties and nineties, and now what? The New Enlightenment, or the Brave New World? I don't know, but I will be part of it, working to shape it magically for the benefit of all life and spirit in the Freedom of the Goddess and in her warm arms.

THE BIRTHDAY

Celebrate this birthday with a giveaway. It has probably been far too long since you cleared out your shelves and drawers. You've entered a new stage of life, and there are things you don't need anymore. If your friends absolutely insist on bringing you something, tell them they can supply the food and flowers. As your friends choose each gift, share its history—where you got it, when you wore it, read it, used it—what it means to you.

Sixty-two

CONGRATULATIONS! At this point you're definitely sliding off the hinge between the second and third missions. Your starwork now is to be patient and observe your new destiny unfolding. It is going to take awhile.

Many respond to these changes with a renewed sense of personal direction. To their surprise, they feel younger. Even those who felt their lives were over may discover opportunities for new achievement. At sixty-two, the newly widowed Eleanor Roosevelt became the first United States representative to the United Nations and chaired the Human Rights Commission, becoming the main force behind the creation of the Universal Declaration of Human Rights that was ratified two years later.

How you feel may depend on your body, but it also depends on your attitude. Are you going to experience this decade as a time of physical ossification and psychological death, or a time of transition into the age of wisdom?

Z recalls:

> I celebrated my sixtieth birthday with a huge party, but my body was in pain. I didn't leave my chair all evening. My leg hurt from the shins to the thighs and no amount of massage helped. It took me until age sixty-two to discover I was wearing the wrong shoes. For two years I had been like a deer caught in the headlights, numb and defeated. I didn't mind aging, but the loss of mobility hurt my soul as well as my body. I spent a lot of money on a variety of specialists until I found a podiatrist who suggested new shoes. She put a little lift into my shoe and all the pain unraveled and faded away like a bad nightmare at dawn. I hope all my problems will be solved this easily, and I hope it won't take this long to stumble upon a solution!

The Birthday

Let your light shine! Set out all sixty-two candles on a tray on a table (covered with fire-resistant material). You can stick little birthday candles upright or for a real blaze, use tea lights, which come in their own metal holders. Make the candles the centerpiece for an altar that honors your life. Decorate it with flowers.

Let the candles burn while you eat your birthday cake and have a good time with your friends. But before they burn out, go up to the altar and say:

> *It is time, it is time—*
> *hearken to the winds of time.*
> *Let it be, let it shine,*
> *Third Destiny be mine!*
> *Health to my body,*
> *Wealth to my mind,*
> *Wisdom to be happy,*
> *Third Destiny be mine!*

Now blow out all those candles (more than one breath is okay!). When they are out, light a single white candle for the new blessings already on their way. Happy Birthday!

Sixty-three

YOU ARE NOW A YOUNG CRONE—what Z calls the "newly old." This is not easy, especially when you don't understand why inside you still feel younger than forty-five. The spirit has stopped aging—it will grow in wisdom, but so long as you keep it open, it will not grow old.

The release from the old status quo can be so liberating that many newly old people experience a rush of inspiration and creativity. Many artists continue to produce new works. Having endured a number of natural cycles of change and transformation gives you perspective and patience. Many artists and thinkers have done their best work after the second Saturn Return. You have a whole new cycle ahead of you, which will last until the third visit of Saturn and the first return of Uranus in your mid-eighties. What are you going to do with this second adulthood?

It is not only women who begin to sense the interconnectivity of life at this time. We need to be aware that men are also moving beyond the gender-based roles they have played and looking inward, as when Don says:

> I don't remember any other age having a different feel, though I suspect that this is because it's been a long and gradual process. I think that over the years I've gained more trust that things will work out well even when events seem chaotic, and I've become less likely to add to my list of projects without careful thought. I'm probably more tolerant. I tend to see everything as a vast web of interconnected processes. I came in at the middle. Everybody tends to make their own simplifying assumptions about it. I'm definitely less attached to material stuff.

But Z offers a warning:

> Your body and your mind may not be in synch anymore. You cannot take anything for granted. This you must accept with charm and a sense of humor. For instance, I injured myself in my own bed. When it was so cold this winter I put on my bed two extra comforters. At night I toss and turn and kick at the covers, and they were so heavy I hurt my kneecap. I limped for a week until I figured it out, took off the extra covers, and closed the window instead. Such is the plight of the newly old. We are not yet good at it. Pay attention to the body's limits and don't push it over the pain threshold!

THE BIRTHDAY

This year, start over again with your candles. Put three on your cake, one for each year of this new decade. This will impress upon your deep mind that you are just a baby Crone. Your new self is just beginning to emerge, new desires are surfacing. You are starting with a clean slate.

Sixty-four

WILL YOU STILL NEED ME, will you still feed me, when I'm sixty-four?" In the 1960s, sixty-four seemed a long ways off. For those who have now reached that age, things may look very different. Your new destiny might have given you a boost, but by now you may be getting tired. You are the only expert on what you need, and you are responsible for making sure you get it. Life has become something of a science—you have to take your meds and vitamins, remember to do a little yoga, take that daily constitutional. You have to eat right—leafy greens and beets and garlic, and drink enough water, ginkgo biloba, nettle tea. By the time you're done it's evening, and then you need your sleep.

Astrologically speaking, it will be quiet in the skies until next year, so this is a fine time to feel your leftover oats. Make sure you laugh and eat and love every day, and then love some more. Z says:

> *I think that all of us Crones and Cronies (that's a male crone) should have dogs who love us. Exercising the dog gives purpose to our walk. It's also very grounding (Where is that little bag?). A dog will insist on its walk and you cannot blow it off. This way, you too get out every day. My dog Zyna has also learned to cook. I developed this bad habit of burning my food because I would tune out. Now she comes and barks at me when it's time to check the stove. Thank you, Zyna!*

Nina writes:

> *Physically (being this age) hurts. So does a look into a mirror that compels me to really see the wreckage of my once-beautiful self. Falling facial lines and thinning hair and all of the body*

*headed for the floor takes some adjusting to. But having made
the mental rearrangement, I like being past the age of caring so
much what others see in me and being able to be what I am without having anything to prove or needing to impress anyone at all.
I feel very free now, and almost light on my feet, in spirit.... So
much living, so many pleasures and so many pains have taught
me to live in the sunlight and let the darkness take care of itself. I
always had the notion that I must hurry around the next corner
in the path to see what new and different idea or what splendid
person waited there. It has all been a grand adventure, one I am
grateful for.... I may have one lifetime remaining or a hundred
lifetimes. I'll take as many as there are....*

Shez, who lives in England, has some even more inspiring words:

*I used to think that by the time I got to sixty or seventy, I
would know it all. It's only when you reach sixty or seventy that
you realize how much you don't know and how much more there
is to learn.... Many people think that getting old is frightening,
but I am still the same me as I was when I was twenty, just a lot
more experienced and far more patient. Now I have a lot of wrin-
kles, and stretch marks from having children, and my hair is
nearer white than its normal ash blonde, and I could definitely
do with losing quite a few pounds....*

*Being old can be a lot of fun. You get away with stuff you
could never have got away with when you were young. You have a
strong personality and you have confidence in yourself.... No
children hanging around your ankles, you're no longer a wage-
slave, and you have the time to really learn things, improve your
skills, and expand your knowledge.*

THE BIRTHDAY

Make this a thankfulness ritual. Put four candles on your cake—green,
white, yellow, and blue. That's one for each year and for Earth, Air, Fire,
and Water.

Light the green candle and say, "I am thankful for the food I eat and for the body I live in. . . ."

Light the yellow candle and say, "I am thankful for the air I breathe and for words and music. . . ."

Light the red candle and say, "I am thankful for the sun that lights my days and the fire of life within me. . . ."

Light the blue candle and say, "I am thankful for the water I drink and for the blessing of love. . . ."

Say "Thank you," as well, to your friends and family and thank them for their help and support.

Sixty-five

SO, YOU'RE SIXTY-FIVE—ready to retire yet? For the next two years, Saturn will square its natal position, leaving you with the same kind of restlessness you felt when it did the same thing between the ages of thirty-seven and forty-four. It's time to change your self-image, but how? The emphasis now is on focus—on finding your new identity. This may take awhile. Look around, and look within. You may discover newly ripened wisdom in your memory banks. Do you often find yourself giving advice to others? Listen to what you are saying, and then take your own advice! We often tell others what we ourselves need most to hear.

We all grew up with the assumption that sixty-five was the "right" age for retirement. That figure was originally arrived at by the German Chancellor Bismarck, who set it as the age for awarding pensions because statistics showed that a majority of workers would be dead by then. Obviously that is no longer so. Betty Friedan's third book, *The Fountain of Age,* questions the negative mystique that until recently has dominated American thinking about the later years.

These days, if you make it to sixty-five you are likely to be around for another twenty years. Some people "retire" from their first career at fifty and start another. Social Security recognizes the changing demographic by encouraging people to put off the age at which they activate their benefits, and has moved the age at which one starts to collect them to sixty-seven. Of course, those of us who are self-employed never get to retire.

What are you going to do with this new leisure? Well, for one thing, don't assume that Social Security is going to take care of you. Your new job is to create a support system so that you won't fall below the poverty line. Find something worthwhile to fill the place where going to work used to be. It may be another kind of work. Your Third Destiny may bring you not only a new personality, but a new career.

Either way, it's time to choose how we are going to spend our Wisdom years. If, when we look around, we see only limitations, life will become progressively more confined and miserable. But if we take charge of our lives and find a new direction, we will discover that the world still holds opportunities.

Phylicia writes, "I celebrated my last birthday with a camping trip with my dog and then a ritual and party. . . . I visit the chiropractor a whole lot more, but I've never been more content or happy. I've learned to honor and love my old friends and relish the new ones."

Charline also is enjoying her arrival at this age:

> *Well, I turned sixty-five a couple of weeks ago and, y'know what? Other than the fact that I now qualify for Medicare it wasn't that big a deal. . . . It doesn't feel as if I've been around long enough to be sixty-five. I don't mind being old, it's just surprising. But my kids have no business being in their forties. They're still supposed to be twenty-something.*
>
> *One of the things I've discovered is the elasticity of time. I think of 1954, when I graduated from high school; that was forty-eight years ago, but it seems just a few years back. And yet, when I look at the chronology of my life I find great blocks of years when "nothing happened." I can call up "the year my eldest was born" (1956), or "the summer we went to Yellowstone" (1965), and such, but what happened to those decades when life just went on, with no memorable changes?*

*Several years ago I likened my life to a house with many
rooms. Some of the rooms I used regularly; others only occasionally. And there were some that had once been important, but their
doors had been closed for a long time, and probably wouldn't be
opened again. I thought I had explored all the rooms in this
house, and it would just be a matter of good housekeeping from
then on. Then that second Saturn Return rolled around, and I
found to my great surprise that the house not only had rooms I
hadn't even looked into, it had a whole other floor!*

*I've learned that there's always something new to wonder at,
that in the long run you can only depend on yourself and the
gods and sometimes they need persuading, that it takes less
energy to smile than it does to frown, that "an it harm none, do
as thou wilt" is a good way to live, and that very small dogs
make excellent housemates.*

THE BIRTHDAY

It's time to begin discovering your new self with this birthday. Sit down
and make a list of your resources and obligations. Include not only
financial information, but contacts, interests, and skills. To whom do
you owe time or support? What do they owe to you? When you have
done this, make a list of things you have always wanted to do. Is there
anything on your list of resources or obligations that will help you
toward one of these goals? On your birthday, take one step in a new
direction—a visit, a phone call, buying a book. Whether you celebrate
alone or with others, raise your glass and toast your new interest.

Sixty-six

THIS YEAR SATURN IS STILL SQUARING SATURN. The great Teacher is
teasing us, unhinging us, questioning. The greater planets take
awhile to move through our lives. The inner work of self-realization
takes a long and steady effort to accomplish, as does the outer work

of creating a stable lifestyle. We need to be mindful of who and what we are.

The dissatisfaction that Saturn brings can take many forms. For some it may manifest as a denial of aging. For men this may be particularly difficult. They are still physically capable of fatherhood, but are they interested? Both men and women need to realize that sexual performance is no longer a primary determinant of our value. Certainly sex is still possible, desirable, and fun, but it is no longer the top priority. What is growing stronger is the need for intimacy.

As male testosterone levels drop and female levels rise, men and women are becoming more alike, and potentially better able to understand each other. Don't let old habit patterns come between you and your mate. Cuddle, do things together, *talk*. . . . Be aware also that intimacy is no longer so closely tied to sexual orientation. Deepen relationships with friends. Explore your own inner world and develop your mind. Read, discuss, do crossword puzzles. Stand on your head or hang over the edge of a chair or sofa to get the blood flowing back to your brain!

Heggaia is a good example of a man who has found a way to revitalize his life in his sixties:

> *What feels weird (about being sixty-six) is being alive in 2001 when HAL (the computer in the film 2001) didn't make it. As an adolescent, I never believed I would live into the twenty-first century and see Buck Rogers. . . . When I retired from state service my wife asked me what I would do to keep busy and out from underfoot. I went back to school, got a second Ph.D., and am starting a new career as a clinical psychologist.*

Sixty-seven

THIS YEAR YOUR PLANETS ARE IN MOTION ONCE MORE, so get ready. Saturn is now in opposition to his natal point, and we will be feeling some conflicts. Our spirits still feel young, but our bodies may have another opinion. Aches and twinges, or a simple desire to take more naps, change our concept of what we can and cannot do. Even if we have kept in shape, we may have to make adjustments. Kneecaps are becoming more fragile, and jogging may no longer be an option. A lifetime of bad posture may be taking its toll on the spine. Breast health is another issue, and at this age, women need yearly mammograms.

For others the conflicts may involve relationships in the family. Some are dealing with older parents while others are being dealt with by their children. Saturn brings some frugality into the picture, especially relevant for those who are on a fixed income. Even the most contented or self-controlled person can fall into depression if we become preoccupied with death and aging, worry about no longer being needed, let death or divorce devastate us. We have to go through the pain without trying to deny or repress it. If we hold back, the pain can make us physically sick. Denied issues have a way of surfacing as aches and pains or even fevers.

Pain and ill health may make life difficult, but they need not prevent it from being productive. For Marie Curie, work in her laboratory made life worthwhile to the end, even though it was her frequent exposure to radiation that undoubtedly brought on her early death from leukemia. Sometimes a trade-off between quality and length of life is necessary.

Women tend to react to stress by seeking the support of friends, whereas men are more likely to retreat from contact and try to go it alone. Now is the time to renew your bonds with others. Join a group, look for adventures that will jolt you out of your rut, or take advantage of opportunities to seek therapy.

Try to mellow out. Even those who have been super-active during most of their lives may find it's time to kick back and watch the flowers grow. Now is when we choose how to approach our Cronehood. We can take the steps needed to maintain physical, mental, creative, social, and spiritual health, or we can give up and be miserable until we die.

Don't just sit there and eat your pain. Go deep within and search for self-healing. These days, the healing traditions of many cultures are available to us if we choose to explore them. Whatever we do, changes are coming. The best approach is to go with the flow.

Annie says that at sixty-seven, "I feel really good; I am a healthy woman—and I know how lucky I am to be here. So, it's okay. *But* I have a lot of *resistance* to aging. What I have learned about life is that this moment is important—just living this one moment now. I am 'getting better' at this, and it is so gratifying and wondrous. Live in this very moment—that's really *all* you can do."

We need to let Saturn's energy carry us through some soul-searching and re-evaluation. What is real? What do we really need? It's time to get rid of those things, and those relationships, that are doing us no good. It is also time to let go of old resentments by forgiving those who have hurt us, and get rid of guilt by making amends to those we may have harmed.

THE BIRTHDAY

Let this birthday become an opportunity to make or renew connections. Phone or write to as many friends from the past as you can find, especially the ones you have neglected because of work or distance. Compare notes, offer congratulations or sympathy as needed, and don't lose touch with them again.

This is also a time to settle any family feuds and have a serious talk with your children about their reactions to your parenting. Let them know that you are open to hearing about any resentments or complaints they may have. You did the best you could at the time, but no one is perfect. By now they will have made enough mistakes themselves to be more accepting of yours, once they understand.

Sixty-eight

GETTING OLDER? WE'RE IN GOOD COMPANY. As life expectancy extends, the proportion of people living on Earth who are over sixty will increase until there are more of us than ever before. Just as a Youth Culture emerged in the mid-twentieth century, a Senior Culture is developing now. We are living longer, healthier lives, and can stay active to a much later age than people did in the past. In many ways we are a pioneer generation. The Gray Panthers started this work—it is up to us to continue it.

Creative people don't have to worry about retirement—they keep on working until they drop, pen or brush still in hand. But if we have passed our mid-sixties, we'll probably be around for a while. We are either retired or looking forward to retirement. A brief rest may be an attractive idea, but pretty soon we'll be looking for something new. At this time we may find ourselves re-energized.

If we are active, it's a good time to travel, while we can still walk around and take in the sights. See the world, visit spas and hot springs, and submerge your body in mineral baths. Seek the company of younger people and do some volunteer work. We may envy their strong bodies, but we'll be grateful for our own emotional maturity. Teaching someone to read and write or doing other charity work can be highly rewarding. Invest in the work of a young artist.

As Molly's mother puts it:

> *I wouldn't trade the content of my head and my heart for a younger body. The older you get, the more obvious it is that your life is unfolding on schedule, according to the plan of your higher self, the gods, or whatever, regardless of what you thought the agenda was—leading you kicking and screaming toward your authentic self and a fully actualized life. The good news: You never need to figure anything out or make anything happen—just stay receptive to your dreams and intuition, and watch the miracles unfold before your eyes. As you merge consciousness with Spirit or the gods, or, in my case, the Bodhisattva Kuan Yin, you rely on this source and not other humans to fill you—a state of detached compassion and peace.*

THE BIRTHDAY

Take a trip to some place you have always wanted to see. This doesn't have to be that journey to Europe that you have always dreamed of, although if it's possible, you should take, or make, the opportunity. But there must be some place within a day's drive that you have always wanted to visit. Go with a friend or go alone. Treat yourself to a good dinner, a show, a massage, or a mud bath. Make it a birthday to remember!

Sixty-nine

T HIS IS THE YEAR WE SMELL THE ROSES. Take some time off to experience joy. If the capacity to experience delight has been worn out of us by the years, it's time to learn how all over again. The ability to feel joyful is part of our birthright—the stars dance, and so should we! This may or may not involve physical dancing, but it can—our friend Laurie's mom was winning ballroom dance competitions all the way through her seventies. Common sense will tell us whether we should be dancing with our feet or our hearts.

If we found a new destiny during our third Saturn Return, we will already be ten years into it. If we are still dreaming about that third mission, it's time to plant the seeds and get started. Z's idol Elizabeth Cady Stanton began her career as a public speaker and activist for women's rights at this age. She began to compile the *Encyclopedia of Women's Suffrage,* and traveled through heat or snow in horse-drawn carriages to persuade people how essential it was to give the vote to women. She carried on with this work for twenty years, and eventually became so famous that the City of New York closed down for a day in her honor and celebrated her life with a ceremony at Carnegie Hall.

We are moving into the time of harvest, in which we reap the good deeds and friendships we have sown. The relationships we establish now will create the families on which we depend when we become official, card-carrying Elders. Each destiny adds new family members to those we inherit from the past, but we get to choose the families of our Third Destiny.

Z's Aunt Titi has neighbors who adopted her when she was in her sixties. As she says:

Hungarians lost most of her generation in the war. There are very few old people left. These countries are very young. So the young couple who live next door started looking after Aunt Titi. This came in very handy when Aunti broke her good arm and could not help herself at all. These unrelated neighbors cared for her with great devotion, as if she were their own blood. I am very grateful, because had they not done so, I would have had to move back to the old country and look after her personally, since I am the last relative of hers left.

THE BIRTHDAY

Spend this birthday with your Third Destiny family. If your blood relatives don't live in the same town, don't worry. Invite the people you live and love and work with now. Let them know you care about them—and give them the chance to show they care about you!

Seventy

ANOTHER DECADE HAS BEEN ACHIEVED! We can draw a deep breath and take stock of our lives. For many this will be a good year, full of activity. For others, it may be time to slow down a little, recognize the body's limitations and allow help to come into our lives. Others are still going strong—in 2001, seventy-year-old Viktor Korchnoi beat a twenty-five-year-old in the Biel International Chess Tournament.

We need to pass on what we've learned. Make yourself available as a mentor, take on an intern or an apprentice. Let's do a better job than our elders did informing the young about how to live and love and die. This gift is now in our grasp. At seventy, like it or not, we are cast in the role of sage. In fact, for many Third Destiny people, this is a turning point.

After a conventional life as a housewife and mother, Grandma Moses took up painting and had the first show of her work at this age. After that, her creativity skyrocketed, and she had a full, successful career that made her a household word. Men can also do an about-face at this time. Z recalls meeting a young man at a conference who told her that when his father, who had been an angry, John Birch–style conservative, reached seventy, he changed, became a great advocate on behalf of children, and even became pro-Choice. He campaigned for causes with great success, testified in Congress and talked to senators. He had another eighteen years to fulfill a Third Destiny in which he championed the young and the poor. His son was baffled and delighted at the same time, and they became closer than they had ever been before.

If you are already well launched on your third mission, keep up the good work. But take time to play as well. Use your energy to mingle, to touch, and to embrace. Keep your brain young by studying a new language or doing crossword puzzles. But remember to take care of your body as well. Adopt the custom of a daily nap. In Europe they lie down around noon and don't get up until 2:30. Then they eat a little, have coffee, and finish the day. If you nap, you can afford to stay up late and watch those old movies you missed the first time around!

THE BIRTHDAY

This is a milestone! Don't let it go by unheralded. Celebrate with a good meal at a restaurant and a trip to the opera or the theater or a sports event you'll enjoy. If you are alone, log on to a chat room and announce your birthday. Make sure you have places to go and people to talk to.

Are you getting tired of the old "Happy Birthday" song? Try saluting your birthday Swedish style, with the "Födelsdagssången" or "Beginning day song." The tune is traditional, slightly adapted. In English, it goes:

> *Yes, may she live, yes, may she live,*
> *Yes, may she live to her hundredth year!*
> *Yes, surely, she'll live, yes, surely, she'll live,*
> *Yes, surely, she'll live to her hundredth year!*
> *And when she has lived, and when she has lived*

And when she has lived to her hundredth year,
Then we'll trundle her out, then we'll trundle her out
Then we'll trundle her out in this wheelbarrow here!

Yes, may she live, yes, may she live, yes, may she live to her hun - dredth year! Yes sure - ly she'll live, yes sure - ly she'll live, yes sure - ly she'll live un - til her hun - dredth year! And when she has lived, and when she has lived, and when she has lived un - to her hun - dredth year, then we'll trun - dle her out, then we'll trun - dle her out, then we'll trun - dle her out in this wheel - bar - row here!

Finish with four sharp "Hurrahs!"

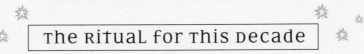

The Ritual for This Decade

BECOMING AN ELDER

When Z decided it was time for a Croning Ritual, she held it at the Fire Circle at the campground that is the setting for the Goddess Conference. While the bonfire swirled sparks to mingle with the stars, she moved in a circle around it, supported by the love of women of all ages who were watching. With their support, Z said good-bye to her old life and embraced the new. It was a dramatic scene, but the essential symbolism can be reproduced much more simply.

Your first decision is to choose the right moment to announce your transition into the third stage of life. Menopause comes when your body decides it is time to give up the possibility of motherhood, and your second Saturn Return is determined by the inevitable planetary orbit. But the best time to declare yourself an Elder (or, if you prefer, Wisewoman or Sage), is up to you. For some, this will be when the physical and emotional changes of menopause are completed. Others will want to wait until the Saturn Return is completed and the nature of the Third Destiny is becoming clear. The social changes that come with retirement and beginning Social Security are the signal for others. Or there may simply come a time when you realize that there has been a change in your perspective, and you want to honor your inner transformation with a celebration for members of your family or friends.

Most of us have at least a few friends with whom we would wish to share this moment—one of the functions of ritual is to change the relationship between an individual and a community. But that relationship will alter whether or not there is anyone present to witness the moment in which you accept the change. In the Anglican Church, a sacrament is defined as an outward and visible sign of an inward and invisible grace. If necessary, you can perform these ritual actions alone as a dialogue between your conscious and unconscious minds.

If the season and circumstances permit, reserve a space in a public park where you can have a bonfire. Or, if you prefer, you can prepare a tray with a candle for each year of your life and set it (on a heatproof pad) in the center of the room.

Wear your favorite color and a wreath of green leaves or flowers. Fill a basket with tokens of your first adult life. They could include a photo of yourself with your small children, papers from work, mementos from trips you have taken, or tokens of hobbies in which you have lost interest, even, perhaps, some symbols of things you loved to do but recognize you no longer can.

When you come in, your guests will clap and greet you. Thank them for coming to witness your transformation. Explain that you still love them, as you love your life, but that there are things you need to release in order to move on.

Imagine that the circle you are making around the fire is the circle of life. As you complete the first third, think about your childhood and youth, and what your memories of that time mean to you now. If you are able, you may say a few words about these things. If any of your tokens relate to those years, cast them into the fire or into a box near the tray of candles. Now cover the second third of your life, and think, or talk, about the mission of your Second Destiny. What were your hopes, your successes and failures? Cast away the symbols of those concerns until your basket is empty. This can be a very emotional moment. Give yourself time to work through it and if you need to, cry. Last of all, take off your crown of flowers.

Two-thirds of the way around the circle, stop. One or two of your friends can bar the way, and state that the circle of your life is not complete, or you can simply contemplate that realization. Let your guests talk (or think) about the ancient role of older women as culture bearers, and the problems that contemporary culture has with respecting the wisdom of age. You have given up your flower wreath. Instead, let them present you with a wreath of ripe wheat ears (available at florist supply stores).

Wearing the wreath, sit down on a "throne" for the party. Tell stories about your life, especially tales that will surprise or even shock some of your listeners. They may think that because they know your past they know *you*—shake them up a little and keep them guessing. Then talk a bit about your plans for the future!

Even if you must "give birth" to your new Crone self alone, go through the ritual. Write out a description of the things you are giving up, and the things you plan to do. In some ways, a solitary declaration of maturity can be even more effective than a community ritual.

AGES 71 TO 80

The Secret Country

To THOSE WHO HAVE NOT YET REACHED THEM, the years beyond age seventy are an unknown country. Writers talk about the secret world of childhood, but they are mistaken—everyone who becomes an adult has been there, though it may be hard to remember it. It is the later years that are the real mystery. Young Crones watch their elders as once we watched the "Big Kids" in school. "What do you know?" we wonder. "How have you survived?"

In the old days, we valued our elders because there were so few of them. Grandmothers and grandfathers were the carriers of the society's accumulated wisdom and values, and they were the ones who passed that information on to the young. In Iceland, the oldest and most sacred compilation of ancient poetry was called "Edda," which means "great-grandmother." Then the youth culture of the twentieth century did its best to sweep all that was not "modern" away.

But the twenty-first century is likely to see some changes. The youths of the mid-twentieth century are the senior citizens of the twenty-first. In the years to come, elders will be valued because there are so many of us, and we vote! Organizations like the Gray Panthers and the American Association of Retired People have become powerful advocates for senior rights. These days, seventy-two-year-olds define becoming "elderly" as something that will happen in their futures—say, at age eighty-five. As we have seen, the years after retirement are no longer a hiatus before life ends, but the beginning of a new phase of life whose existence was barely glimpsed before.

Improved health care makes longer life not only possible but probable. The question now is what the *quality* of that life will be. New issues confront us—mobility, independence, security. When the college newsletter arrives we look at the back to see who has died. Predators seek to take advantage of our fears. Some of us are taking care of aging parents or mates, while others end up moving in with their children. Genetics, past history, and chance play a large part in deciding how our bodies will react to aging, but they do not determine everything. We may not be able to control all that happens to us, but we can decide how to react to it. Our choices and actions can make the difference between a Third Destiny that is filled with interest and fulfillment and one in which we are just marking time.

FATE DATES FOR AGES 71 TO 80			
Ages 71–74	♄ ☍ ♄	Saturn opposes self	•Unsettled period •Enforced frugality •Old roles outgrown
Age 72	♃ ☌ ♃	Jupiter returns	•Expansive period •Time to mellow out
Age 76	☊ ☋	Moon's nodes return to natal position	•New emotional cycle begins
Age 80	♄ □ ♄	Saturn squares itself	•Can be rewarding •Care versus independence •Quality of life concerns

Seventy-one

CONGRATULATIONS ON DEALING with all the inner changes you have experienced so far! Now it's time to take stock and plan for the changes that lie ahead.

It is common to speak of the body as the temple of the spirit, but in many ways, it's more like a beloved spouse. There are days when you'd like to trade it in for a younger model, but you've been through so much together, and you understand each other so well! Really, you're better off taking care of each other.

So, what nice thing have you done for your body lately? You have to give it some downtime, a chance to renew. In Europe, the tradition is to "take the waters" at one of the hot springs or spas that have always been places of healing. In America, spas are not such an integral part of the culture, but there are many places where you can frolic in the water while getting a cure. You need to waterlog on minerals. Supported by water, you can exercise safely. If you can't go to a hot spring, you can benefit from aqua-aerobics at the local YMCA or public pool.

Give your body half a day and let your spirit take the other half. Allow time for creative work and for play. But unless your body is in a full cast, don't sit and watch television all day! Turn off the tube and go for a walk. Listen to the planet. If you are hurting, take the best painkillers you have and get out of the house. Many of our diseases cannot yet be cured, but we have some dynamite medications to mask the symptoms. Don't be too proud to use them. Life is too short to waste a moment on unnecessary suffering.

If you are working on your third mission, hit it hard this year. But start training an apprentice as well. Having a right-hand man or woman will provide some support and another pair of shoulders to take the strain. You still have a destiny, but you are no longer responsible for everything.

THE BIRTHDAY

Do some research and find out the location of the nearest hot springs or spa. Then call up a friend and arrange to soak in the pools on your birthday. Tell friends who want to give you birthday presents to contribute to the expedition. One can help pay for the gas to get there. Another can chip in for a good massage. As you soak in the healing water, imagine all your aches and pains dissolving away. Tell your body how much you love and depend on it. You are giving it this present of comfort and healing, and expect that in return it will carry you safely through the coming year.

Seventy-two

THIS YEAR, THE SKIES HAVE SOME GIFTS and surprises in store. This is also one of the years in which Jupiter returns, opening up new horizons, and bringing you some energy. Your emotions are changing now, growing deeper. If you were always reserved, you may find yourself becoming more outgoing. On the other hand, those who were always the life of the party may discover hidden depths that they need to explore. You may have turned into your own opposite—can you love this changed self? Can you embrace the older you and accept her without bitterness? Can you even celebrate the change?

Many people of this age are in denial. They wish to be young so they marry someone younger. For a while this may provide new energy, but in time the fix fails. It's better to bond with people of our own generation than to chase youth. One form of exercise and entertainment that is both safe and fulfilling is singing. Singing heals the spirit and gives the body a chance to play with breath and sound. Developing the older voice will make it more beautiful. Breathing deeply fills the body with energy while sweet sounds invigorate the spirit. Singing with others is a way to make human contact. Sing by yourself, and if you can, join a choir.

We have to recognize that being older can be a struggle. One of the key issues is the fight to retain independence. This is why it is important to start planning for retirement when you are younger, and to take full advantage of senior discounts and assistance programs. Patricia, who is seventy-two, lives in a trailer in a nice area near a lake.

But Social Security doesn't quite cover her expenses, so she needs to clean house for some ladies older and more disabled than she is. She gets some free meals at the senior center and from the churches. She has a roommate, a man in his forties, who helps her a lot around the house. Sometimes, when she is depressed, she drinks—for those who have lost money, friends, and mates, alcoholism can be a real threat.

She says, "I feel just the same as I always did! I feel like I am only in my forties, and then I look in the mirror and I don't recognize myself. I say, 'Who is that old lady looking back at me?' I have to keep on working, I can't afford to eat if I don't." However she finds her two dogs and her cat a comfort. All of them adore her. She feeds them chicken in broth she cooks herself and grates carrots into. "My babies get food that is as good as mine because they are people too." They sleep in her bed with her, and the dogs go with her even when she cleans for her ladies. She has no interest in another husband—"What would I want with a dirty smelly old man that I would just have to pick up after and be taking orders from all the time? At my age the old men just want a nurse and housekeeper, but they call it a wife."

One way to deal with depression is laughter. The act of laughing stimulates the immune system and relieves stress—whether or not you actually think of anything funny. Take a deep breath and release it in a series of "Ho, ho, ho's." Soon you will be smiling, if only because you feel so ridiculous. Laughter really is the best medicine.

THE BIRTHDAY

This year, celebrate sound and breath. This is your sixth dozen year, so put twelve blue candles on your cake and a white one for the year to come. Take a deep breath and blow them all out at once. Invite some friends over and see how many old songs you all know.

Seventy-three

THE THEME FOR THIS YEAR IS, "Reap what you have sown!" Make some opportunities to sit back and take stock. Your spirit may still feel young, but you need to keep an eye on your body. If you have been putting off getting a checkup, now is the time to schedule one. However, new studies suggest that the risk of breast cancer goes down after seventy, and you may not need such frequent mammograms. Consult with your doctor regarding the right timing for you.

Consider also what you have given to the world and what you still have to give. Give some time, money, or energy to a good cause. If you can afford to help sponsor a young artist or activist, do so. If not with money, you can help with publicity or networking. Get your portrait painted.

If you are wondering how to exercise without hurting yourself, find someone who is teaching very gentle, beginner's yoga. Stretch, and lengthen your spine. If you can't stand on your head, let it hang down for a few minutes each day to flush the brain with blood. Stimulate your mind by reading something that challenges you.

Attitude can make a big difference. Julie, who will be seventy-three soon, says being this age is terrific!

> *Fortunately, I'm an artist, both theatrical and in original crafts. As a category, such people simply do not retire—ever. To us our work is life—not a dirty word. George Burns, pushing ninety, advised, "Find a reason to get up in the morning!" This, after losing his life's partner, Gracie Allen, in the '50s. Jon Peerce, the great leading Metropolitan Opera tenor, was still recording for Columbia Records in his eighties. At the same age, Pablo Casals gave command cello concerts at the Kennedy White House. Licia Albinese, though no longer singing, is staging and directing operas in her nineties. And did Pablo Picasso ever really quit?*

THE BIRTHDAY

If your living situation allows, get a pet to look after and keep you company. A dog is a good companion. When you have to get out to walk the dog every day you cannot put off getting your exercise. Dogs are devoted and nonjudgmental. With a dog, you will never be lonely.

Seventy-four

THIS YEAR, SATURN WILL BE OPPOSING his natal position in your chart most strongly, which is always a source of strain. You may be especially vulnerable to accidents, or there may be other physical problems. Avoid unnecessary operations and be careful with your health. At this time you may find yourself feeling lonely and insecure. The best solution is to stay physically conservative while becoming a spiritual adventurer. You need to change how you see yourself in relation to the larger world. This year, stay close to home. Enjoy moderate exercise but don't push it. Play with your own grandchildren or become an adopted granny for others. There are far too many children in this world whose lives, either because of distance or estrangement, don't include an effective grandparent.

Leigh says she would rather still be seventy. She has the following advice: "Never stop learning; stay on the sunny side of life, support your children with love; love between the sexes does not last; violence begets violence—stop the war."

This is a good age to get busy with projects. If you have taken care of your body you can still do a lot of work. Listen to your soul and discover what she would still like to do. To live happily and healthily we have to do something we love—gardening, helping others, teaching one's children or grandchildren, taking care of animals. Loving keeps the spirit young.

Z and Diana both attend yoga classes at the Berkeley Senior Center, striving to become as flexible as women twenty years older than they. Pondurenga, the teacher, still rides his bike all over town. He can twist his body like a pretzel and he laughs a lot, even though his circulation is not as good as it used to be because he "drives on one less cylinder in his heart." He finds being seventy-four surprising. "I notice things failing, yet some problems are still reversible. [I have learned] to replace fear, anger and annoyance with curiosity. There is more than enough sadness and rage. Be happy for no reason!"

THE BIRTHDAY

Let your theme for this birthday be "All you need is love!" Choose to spend it with those you love and who love you. Will it make you happiest to let your friends take you out to dinner, or would you rather choose to make others happy by giving them a treat? There is joy both in giving and receiving.

Seventy-five

THREE-QUARTERS OF A CENTURY! That's an achievement, surely—so make this a year of celebration. Make room to enjoy life by simplifying it. Look at your living situation—can your house be changed so that it is easier to take care of and get around in, or do you need to consider moving to a smaller, simpler place? Are there things cluttering up the place that you haven't used for years and are unlikely to use again? Get rid of them.

With less to take care of, you'll have more time for fun. Make your meals simple, but include lots of variety—red beets and white cauliflower and green beans—different colors and tastes so that you won't get bored. Try some new activities as well. Keep within your comfort levels, but don't lose your curiosity, and don't let yourself be imprisoned by fear. Fear is a tool to keep people in their places. Insist on the freedom and free time to contemplate the beauty of life, and allow time for your mind to wander—who knows where the journey will end?

Allow time for a social life as well. Many seniors like to go on cruises and meet others. There are many stories of people who meet and marry their long-lost loves, or who simply move in with new loves in order to share resources and companionship. Love, whenever it finds you, is precious. But be careful. Seniors are the age group among whom rates for sexually transmitted diseases are rising most quickly. AIDS knows no age barriers. Avoid unprotected sex as if you were twenty years old.

THE BIRTHDAY

Congratulations! This is your Platinum Birthday, to match the strands that glisten in your hair. Time for another big party. For years you may have ignored your birthdays, but you'll find that as you grow older, they become as important to your family and friends as they were when you were a child. If they are lucky, one day they will stand where you do now. One of the duties of an Elder is to show the way. So put up with it—wear purple, and tell a story for every one of the candles on your cake!

Seventy-six

THIS YEAR THE NODES OF THE MOON move back into their natal position. Your emotional self has completed another cycle and is ready to begin a new shift that will carry you to age ninety-five. A moon curve can take you to wonderful peaceful places. Open your heart and let the world in. Allow yourself to love, and then love some more.

More and more, you are learning to live in the moment, and as you do so, you recapture some of the ability to enjoy what each moment brings that you had as a child. Look for opportunities to be around children. Now you can appreciate the brightness of their souls as never before. They've been born into difficult times. Tell them what it was like when you were a child.

Diana remembers that when her grandmother talked about "The War," it was the *Civil* War. "When we would drive by the '76' gasoline sign I would say it was in honor of her. She told me that when she was a little girl she made herself a hoop skirt from some rope and old barrel staves. Stories like that gave me a sense of continuity, an awareness that I was part of a history that stretched back into the nineteenth century."

Use your experience to work on behalf of children as well. Contribute to advocacy campaigns—send out fliers, make phone calls. You are articulate, and if you manage your energy well you can do a great deal.

For people with a pure passion, this age is prime time to do some good in the world. Creative people who put off getting involved in the arts until their Third Destiny may just be hitting their stride. Many writers have done great work at this age.

Of course, the only way to get all this done is to look after your health. Spend half the day taking care of your body and the other half working. Walk, join a senior yoga class. If you can, get a monthly massage. Stretch in the water and swim.

THE BIRTHDAY

Celebrate the child within you! If you have pictures of yourself as a child, display them at your party. Encourage your guests to bring pictures of themselves as children, and try to guess who's who. On the cake, put numeral candles or seven in one color and six of the other. Offer little toys as party favors. Better still, have a picnic at a park where there is a carousel that includes benches as well as animals and ride the merry-go-round. As you go round and round, think of the cycle of life, and count each circle as a year.

Seventy-seven

IN TRADITIONAL AFRICAN SOCIETIES, you have to live to be at least seventy-seven to become an *egungun,* an ancestral spirit, after you die. So congratulations on qualifying as a real Elder. Now your job is to become a good one. None of the great planetary cycles are directly impacting you this year, so you can pay attention to working out your personal destiny.

The key to a good life is balance. You need to take care of your health without letting it dominate your life. Get regular exercise. Avoid taking too many medicines, and check out herbal remedies. Z swears by nettle tea, which she drinks daily. It is very pleasant and will give you vitamins and minerals in a form in which you can absorb them. She sneaks a little jasmine tea into it, too, both for its healing properties and to get a little shot of caffeine.

Take care of your mental health as well—if you feel depressed, get someone to help you analyze your problems. If they are real, take steps to solve them. If not, work on changing your thinking. Try to counter each dark thought with a bright one, and for everything that makes you angry, look for something that pleases you. Especially avoid blaming other people for your problems. Listen to good music and surround yourself with bright colors. If depression persists, try getting more exercise, more daylight, or take a little St. John's Wort. If it remains a problem, talk to your doctor. Negative feelings can poison your body as well as your soul.

Working for the good of others is good for you. Eleanor Roosevelt continued into her seventies to be active in promoting social causes. When she was seventy-seven, President Kennedy appointed her to chair his Commission on the Status of Women.

One place where you can get involved in a positive way is your church or religious organization. Choose a group with a positive attitude that will help you develop your spiritual life as well as doing good works. But if religious people get aggressive about trying to recruit you, investigate them thoroughly—they may be after your money.

If you haven't already done so, you should also be checking out your community's programs for seniors. Take advantage of classes and outings. Offer to teach one yourself. If there is nothing available, gather your friends together and start one. The friends you cultivate now will be your greatest treasure as time goes on.

THE BIRTHDAY

You can celebrate this birthday quietly, but make it an opportunity to give thanks for what you have and begin working to become a worthy ancestor. Honor your own relations who have passed on and invite them to celebrate with you—arrange their pictures, or pictures of people who remind you of them, on a white linen cloth. Place some flowers and a candle before them.

Light the candles on your cake from the candle that is burning for the ancestors, and say, "Your light is my light, my light is your light, from the past to the future and back again. . . ." Make finding out more about your own ancestors this year's project. Learn to see yourself as a link in a very long chain.

Seventy-eight

THE BIG PLANETS ARE STILL giving you a rest, so make this year an opportunity to develop your mind. This could be one of your best years—you are old enough now to say what you think and get away with it. You know what you want. All you have to do is get organized and go after it.

Current research indicates that most of our mental powers—language skills, I.Q., abstract thinking, and verbal expression—continue to stay strong as we grow older. We may think more slowly, but age and experience give us a better ability to see the context of a problem and suggest a wise solution. The major problem is with long-term memory; our minds are like our bookcases—after a while they get full. But in compensation, we can learn to use both sides of our brain. Our brains now process information differently, and with the right stimulation, can even grow new neurons.

It's important to keep on learning and stretching our minds. Learn a new language, memorize great prose or poetry, a few lines more each day. Go to the theater or concerts, or take up painting to develop other areas of the brain. Above all, cultivate your curiosity.

"A sound mind in a sound body" makes sense now too. A healthy brain needs good circulation, so exercise and watch your diet. Spend a few minutes a day with your head below your knees. Vitamins, especially the B-vitamins and anti-oxidants such as vitamin E, seem to offer some protection, and a little coffee from time to time will pep you up too.

But Nature may be your best medicine. Walk in the park. Smell the roses. If you don't have a garden to work in, cultivate potted plants—sinking your fingers into rich soil can bring healing.

THE BIRTHDAY

Start your program of mind expansion on your birthday with an outing to a concert or the theater. If people want to give you presents, ask for books. Sign up for a class or draw up a study plan.

Seventy-nine

B Y NOW YOU ARE THREE-QUARTERS of the way through your Third Destiny. If it has brought you a fulfilling mission, that mission will probably have kept you happy and healthy as well. "Keeping busy" is all very well, but busywork is not a mission. A mission results when the desire of the heart is manifested in action.

Those who are reaching their late seventies today came of age just in time for the Second World War, were young adults during the Cold War, saw their own children go off to Vietnam or protest it in the '60s, and have lived through all the ups and downs since then. Those who reach this age during the next twenty years will also bear the burden of the decisions made during the second half of the twentieth century. We are the ones who voted the leaders of the past fifty years into power, or failed to stop them. What kind of a world are we leaving to our descendents?

You still have a vote, and at this point, you have far less to lose by taking a stand for your beliefs. You may not be up to marching in the streets, but you can advise those who are. The sub-age of Aquarius is upon us, and its influence is deepening, pushing us to realize our full humanity. The end of the Piscean Age in the early twenty-second century will reveal the positive aspects of the sign—creativity, compassion, love, and transcendence.

One good example of a woman who has always lived life to the fullest is Elizabeth, who taught her teenaged niece about reincarnation and karma, séances and ouija boards, led an exercise class for women who have had mastectomies, and has served on her local school board. She said that she enjoyed answering our questions because it enabled her to dig down deep to try to express some of the things she has felt about her life.

She writes:

> I will be celebrating my eightieth birthday in July. As to how I feel about being that age, I don't really dwell on it. I'm too busy. My body, aside from arthritic problems, is holding up as well as can be expected for a person who has undergone a mastectomy (thirty-three years ago) and a knee replacement. My general health is excellent so those almost eighty years don't interfere with carrying on a very active life. They just give me an added bonus of better judgment as to what I can do, and with whom I choose to spend my time.

> When I let the word eighty enter my consciousness, I don't expend much introspective thought regarding the implications of having lived that many years. When I look back upon those years, the myriad people I've met, the sometimes challenging and exciting things I've done, and the pain and pleasure I've experienced during those times, I attempt to highlight the really significant episodes. In doing so, I feel the warmth of the people I recall. The love and mutual support that I've received from friends and family in those recollections stand out like beacons among my memories.

> I suppose you could say that I've learned that love is the greatest gift I've received in life and the greatest gift I've been able to give. Love can be expressed in many forms—affection and concern for your family and friends, and contributing to the good of your community to meet the needs of those who are less fortunate.

> All in all, nearly eighty years has meant a long time to learn, and since my philosophy encompasses the idea that that is what we're here for, I think my lesson book is nearly filled, and I've never regretted any of the difficult assignments I've received.

THE BIRTHDAY

On this birthday, make the decision to put your beliefs into practice and pass on some of your wisdom. While others are giving presents to you, offer some support, either in time or money, to a cause you believe in. Choose someone younger—someone you can consider your child or grandchild by blood or in spirit, and arrange to go out to lunch or dinner. Find an opportunity to tell her (or him) at least one story that expresses some insight that your life has brought you. Are you thinking that no one will be interested? Sincerity is always compelling, and if your story is important to you, your guest will remember it.

Eighty

GUESS WHO'S BACK? The great teacher, Saturn, is squaring his natal position on his way back toward his third return at age eighty-four. What are you learning this time?

One lesson may be a renewed focus on your health. Has Saturn clipped a little bit more of your energy? Don't despair. Take some time to rest up. You are entering a "sage" zone. The years between now and eighty-four may be a little rocky, but if you can make it till then, you'll get a second wind and a renewal. So get smart and take care of yourself. See your doctor regularly, but take responsibility for your own health, and investigate the many publications on alternative treatments as well. Take herbal teas and exercise! For your body, that's about all you can do.

For your spirit, family ties are very important now. Keep in contact with family members, or adopt some younger folks who are separated or estranged from their own parents. If you have grandchildren who are grown, or nearly, invite them to dinner or on an outing. They should be just the right age to give you the help you need.

But don't depend entirely on family. Your church or religious group and your friends can do a lot to enrich your life. This is certainly true for Dorothea, who lives with her two cats in the house where she raised her children and has lived for the past thirty-seven years. She says that being eighty doesn't feel any different from being seventy-nine, though she realizes she's getting up there. On the other hand, her mother lived to be eighty-seven, so she expects to be around for a while.

As for what she has learned, first, it's important to live one day at a time. Her church is very important—as she says, we all need something to live by, and faith will help get us through the bad times. Until recently, she competed in ballroom dancing and won a number of prizes. She is happiest when she is dancing or listening to music, or when she is with her family, though she doesn't get to see her daughters as often as she would like. Having shared interests is the best way to get along with other people. The other secret is to learn to think before you speak, because it's so easy to open your mouth and put both feet in, which causes strife. The world would be better off if everybody would get back to decent values, and live by them.

THE BIRTHDAY

This is an important birthday. Take the opportunity to do something exciting, if possible with your family. Diana's grandmother celebrated by taking her first helicopter ride from San Pedro to Disneyland. Some of her grandchildren rode with her, and the family spent the day at Disneyland.

What have you always wanted to do that never seemed possible before? Is there some place you'd like to visit, a food you've always wanted to eat, or a show you never got to see? Tell someone—they'll probably be delighted to know what would please you. Or grab a friend and head off on your own adventure. Every year is precious—do what you want to do while you can!

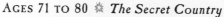

The Ritual for This Decade

CREATING A SPIRITUAL FAMILY

Just as we needed our families to love and support us when we were children, as elders we need relationships and relations. But some of us never married or never had children. Others have children whose lives have taken them far away, either geographically or emotionally. Sometimes, our blood families are near, but the relationship is haunted by unresolved conflicts. We need to be loved, but we don't want to lose our independence; we need to love, but fear to repeat old mistakes.

One way to deal with this difficulty is to create a spiritual family, either by transforming our relationship with those to whom we are linked by blood, or by adopting someone who needs us.

The problem with our blood relatives is that we didn't choose them. A spouse can be divorced, but we're stuck with our siblings and children. At worst, families often suffer the emotional equivalent of a legal separation, but the parting is the more painful because there is no public closure. A married couple can re-evaluate their relationship and signal the new commitment by a renewal of vows. Why not do the same with your family, transforming the relationship from an obligation to a choice?

This does involve a certain amount of risk—what if you ask your children to choose you as their mother and they say No? It certainly requires a great deal of honesty. For parent and child, or brother and sister, to ***choose*** each other, they must be willing to open up to each other on an adult level, to admit the truth about the past (or at least to compare perceptions), and seek for something to unite them beyond a habitual and superficial affection.

Of course, there are also risks in establishing a spiritual relationship with a stranger. With blood family, at least, you already know their flaws. Creating a surrogate family is a new idea, and your proposal may be perceived as strange—it may be best to bring it up in a rather joking manner at first to test for reactions. You will have to communicate very clearly just what you do and do not have in mind. If you do have blood relations, it will also be necessary to specify whether the adoption will have any implications for inheritance. And of course, before you can even consider such a course, you will need to find someone worthy of such a relationship and learn to love them. If your heart is big enough, you can have more than one person in your spiritual family at a time.

So, let us assume that you have completed all these preliminaries and dealt with all the requirements. You have asked your relative(s) or friend(s)— you could, for instance, renew your relationship to all your children at once— to enter into an intentional covenant. If your new family member is a blood relation, you will probably want to do this privately, since as far as the world is concerned, you are related already. If you are adopting new family, however, you may want your commitment to be witnessed by other friends.

The ritual should take place at home. Decorate as you would for any family party, but make sure there are candles or a fire on the hearth. If you feel it appropriate, you may begin by citing the relationship between Ruth and Naomi as an example of the way in which a legal relationship can become a spiritual one:

> In the Old Testament, when the widow Naomi decided to go back home to Judea after her husband and sons had died, her daughter-in-law Ruth, who was from Moab, said these words: "Where you go I will go, and where you lodge I will lodge; your people shall be my people, and your God my God; where you die I will die, and there will I be buried. May the Lord do so to me and more also if even death parts me from you" (Ruth 1:16-17).
>
> It is our intention to establish a similar spiritual kinship today.

Standing or sitting together before the fire say something like:

> I call to witness the holy hearthfire (and all of you who have accepted our invitation today) that it is my wish to take (Name) as my (daughter/son/brother/sister/other relative) today. I do this uncompelled by coercion or custom, but freely and in full understanding that this is a relationship of the spirit, created by pure love.

Your new loved one replies in the same form:

> I call to witness the holy hearthfire (and all of you who have accepted our invitation today) that it is my wish to take (Name) as my

(mother/sister/other relative) today. I do this uncompelled by coercion or custom, but freely and in full understanding that this is a relationship of the spirit, created by pure love.

You then take bread and salt and offer it to your new relation, saying something like the following, or whatever vows you have decided on:

> My hearth shall be your hearth, and my table yours if you have need.
> When you laugh I shall share your joy, and when you weep, your tears.
> From this time until life's ending I promise you a (mother's/sister's/relative's) care and love.

Your relation responds with the same words or whatever else is appropriate, and offers you bread and salt as well.

Then the two of you should clasp hands around a goblet of wine or spring water, and lifting it, say together:

> What we have promised, we shall perform. This we pledge in the name of God (or the Goddess, or Holy Love).

Each of you should drink from the goblet in turn, and then pour out the remainder into a bowl set before the hearth (later it can be emptied into the earth in the garden or by the front door).

When the ceremony is done, everyone should share a home-cooked meal and celebration.

AGES 81 TO 90
AND BEYOND
The Age of Enlightenment

WHY DO WE CRINGE AT THE THOUGHT OF AGING? If we didn't grow older, we would be dead! Look at a corpse—it has certainly stopped aging!

Age is a triumph of the body and mind over the wear and tear of time. Rocks deteriorate, but only organic life grows. A mature human being has survived all those years. No matter what our mission is, if we live long enough we will see our causes win, our purposes fulfilled.

When Diana's grandmother was a little girl, her teacher prophesied that humans would never fly, or reach the moon or the heart of Africa. By the time her grandmother died at the age of ninety-four, all of those things had occurred. Who among those who grew up in the '40s or '50s would have imagined that the Iron Curtain could come down? To live long is to triumph over the slow changes of history.

A long life is also a payback for all the effort it has taken to survive disease, disappointment, and wounds to body and mind. Aging is a gentle path that leads slowly homeward to the other side where our relatives await us. Death is the culmination of aging, but it is paradoxically also its reversal. The dead begin a new existence beyond organic life. They reach the end of the Circle of Rebirth and start again. To accept aging is to begin to understand the meaning of life. Resisting it is the way to become an old fool!

FATE DATES FOR AGES 81 TO 90 AND BEYOND			
Age 82	♆ ☍ ♆	Neptune begins to oppose self	
Age 84	♃ ☌ ♃	Jupiter returns	
Ages 84–86	♄ ☌ ♄	Saturn returns	·End of Third Destiny
			·Freedom to die or from fear of death
			·Acceptance of life cycles
	♅ ☌ ♅	Uranus returns	·Completion of soulwork
			·Freedom to be true self
			·Spirituality develops, soul tackles concepts previously unable
Age 95	♀ ☍ ♀	Pluto opposes self	·Time of ultimate transformation

Eighty-one

NINE TIMES NINE IS A MAGICAL NUMBER, the beads in a Buddhist rosary. There are nine Muses, nine Valkyries. It is the number of the sacred sisterhood. As you enter your eighth decade, you are moving into the most spiritual time of life.

By this time you are coasting down the mission curve toward the completion of your Third Destiny. Your fertility curve is a thing of the past. But your mind curve keeps spiraling. Later in this decade, the great planets will move into your life once more, but now you still have leisure to work on things at your own pace, consider what still needs to be finished, and work on it. So get down and groove. Getting excited about something will keep you healthy. Put on your music and wiggle your toes. Enjoy.

Gertrude, who is on her way to eighty-one, says it's not bad. "I'm very happy. I'm healthy except for having macular degeneration. I can't drive or read anymore, but I'm lucky to live in this age where there are books on tape and computers adapted for low-vision people. I go swimming every day and I enjoy going to the Senior Center for Tai Chi, yoga, and trips." She says we should "enjoy life when you are young, don't wait to have fun until you're old. Be friendly and helpful to people."

At this age, Z's Aunt Titi traveled to Israel and spent summers in Germany. She also still walked everywhere. "She insisted on marching across the bridge over the Duna River and refused the cab that I was getting for her. 'I need the walk,' she said. I looked at her in astonishment, because the bridge is quite long. When I visited her she came with me to all the museums, though sometimes she would nap in her chair in the cafeteria while I was looking at the exhibits. She had seen them all many times."

THE BIRTHDAY

Have a birthday for the sacred sisters. Invite eight friends and make nine cakes, each with nine candles. Let each one of you blow out the candles on her cake and share some words of wisdom. Write down what each one says and make copies for everyone.

Eighty-two

THIS YEAR THE PLANET NEPTUNE is in opposition. This will be the only significant Neptune transit in your life, since his cycle takes

246 years to return to the natal position! This may be a time of confusion, but it will also empower your imagination. Use this energy for spiritual work. Practice lucid dreaming. If you are an artist, this will be a period of inspiration. Artists can really take off at this time in their lives, especially if they have someone to help with the heavy work.

Uranus is also moving closer, opening the heart. If you will open your eyes, you can see the miracle in each small thing. Your physical eyes may not be what they were, but your spiritual eyesight has never been better. You are becoming the Wisewoman. But with this new insight comes a responsibility. You need to pass what you have learned to those who will follow you.

Talk to your descendents, either physical or spiritual. Tell them what it feels like to be your age and what you have learned. It's time to write your life story. Every generation needs to resurrect its history. If writing is difficult, make an audiotape—that may be even better, because you will be recording your voice as well as your words. What you write now will be a legacy for the future. By looking back over your life, you can see patterns emerging, understand how you cooperated with the Fates in doing the work of your century. You had a job, and you did it well.

We cherish the records that have been left to us from the past. Z has a diary that was kept by her grandmother, Vilma:

> I only met her once—she died when I was only a toddler, but I have her recollections from childhood until she was eighteen. She left me etchings. She left behind every one of her school certificates and outpourings of love for my father and my aunt. She wrote compulsively. In those days everybody wrote all the time. My grandfather Zoltan wrote short stories and my aunt Julia wrote diaries. Sometimes the whole family would stay home all weekend and write.

Edna has been making a project of collecting and labeling family pictures. She says, "Sometimes my daughter comes over to help me, and sometimes it is one of my grandsons. I was surprised at first that they would care about aunts and uncles and so forth who died before they were born, but they seem to like to hear my stories. My grandson tells me that this way his memory can go back a century, and I tell him that even I am not that old yet, and we laugh."

THE BIRTHDAY

Gather your family together on your birthday and tell stories. You, as guest of honor, can claim the right to talk as much as you want, but it may be fun to recall some events that your children also remember and compare notes. Talk about your own childhood, and tell the stories that you heard from your own parents and grandparents. If you know something about your great-grandparents, your family's collective memory may span two centuries.

Eighty-three

THIS IS A YEAR TO SIT BACK and catch your breath. Take care of yourself and get ready to deal with the changes that are coming soon. It's time to leave the battlefield. No matter how important your mission was, it's drawing to a close. The revolution will have to continue without you. If it's a good cause, it will. Unless you are writing your memoirs, put your attention on the present. Focus on simplifying your life and stimulating your soul. Ride it out. A new wind is coming.

At eighty-three, Z's Aunt Titi had retired from her job as a pharmacist. She settled into the life of a retiree, though she still went into the pharmacy once a week to help out if a young mother needed to stay home, or if somebody needed a break.

As Z says:

> She can still mix a good painkiller from scratch. I sometimes worried that she would make a mistake, but she never has. When I visited her, she was attending workshops about New Age ideas, crystals, and Buddhism, and liked yoga. But what fed her spirit most was going to the little Baroque Church of St. Anne around the corner. We would sit in the pews and she would glance over at

me as we prayed together to the Boldogasszony, who is the old goddess who we identify with the Virgin Mary. Every church in Hungary is dedicated to her.

THE BIRTHDAY

Take this opportunity to visit some place that was important to you in the past. Remember, when you get to this age, you have a right to be a little demanding, so even if it is difficult, insist that arrangements for transportation be made so you can get there. Take a relative, or someone who means a lot to you, and tell them the story of what you did, or felt, or learned, in this place. If you have a photo, compare what it looks like now and then. Then go have a birthday lunch at the nicest restaurant nearby.

Eighty-four

IN YOUR EIGHTY-FOURTH YEAR a conjunction of planetary cycles combine to bring fulfillment, completion, and transformation. Jupiter is back, bringing expansion and energy. Saturn returns for the third time, bringing the work of the Third Destiny to a close. In this year you will have your first Uranus Return, completing a full cycle of development of the soul's individuality. Only now can you consider your persona for this life fully developed. With this foundation, you can seek for new expressions for your essence.

If you get to this birthday, the chances are you are going for your personal best. Congratulations! You have completed the "saging" process and the Wisdom curve. As your Third Destiny begins to draw to a close, you can feel the energy of Uranus blowing in like a brisk new wind. Watch out—it may make you giddy. An inner laughter is building inside you. You may look at life with a new excitement and awakening interest. Unlike Saturn, Uranus is not a taskmaster. He wants to play. Your body may be fragile, but your spirit may suddenly feel very young.

The first change that Z noticed in her Aunt Titi was that Titi had stopped snoring:

> *She used to have a frightful snore, so loud no one could sleep in the same room. At eighty-four, she packed up and came to visit me in California. When she arrived she took a nap and slept as silently as a baby. Her voice also returned. She no longer used the soft voice I remembered from before. She had much more energy. There was also a personality change. Titi always used to have a bite to her. That's gone, too. She still flares up over misunderstandings, but by and large, she's happier than ever before. I feel very blessed that I can see her and talk to her about people in the past that only she knew.*

THE BIRTHDAY

If each day is the first day of the rest of your life, this birthday is the first day of your life with your completed soul. Of course, it may take awhile for all aspects of your transformation to become apparent, but you can begin the process by planning a perfect day—a day that expresses the best that you know how to be. When is the best time to get up? What is your favorite breakfast? Your day plan does not have to be ambitious, but it should be thought out carefully. See a few people who you really care about. Spend some time in prayer or meditation. Have an intimate celebration at home.

Eighty-five

S ATURN AND URANUS HAVE MOVED in and taken charge. The new awareness you glimpsed last year is now fully upon you. What are you going to do with it? These are the planets of individuation, the helpers that enable us to change and mature. Uranus liberates us from restrictions and Saturn defines us. Individuation is a continuing process, but its goal is to unite us with Spirit by completing the realization of that part of us which is a unique but integral part of the Divine.

One of the things this completion can do is to liberate us from the fear of death. For some, indeed, reaching this point is sufficient. They have done what they came to do, and if the body is tired, it becomes easy to let go and go home. Of course, death can come at any age, but astrologically, some times are more conducive to passing on than others. But if you don't die, after this you will get stronger. And you can stop snoring.

You may find that your psyche is becoming more open. You know more about the people around you, but you are also more aware of the invisible world. You may have interesting and vivid dreams of those who have gone before, which leave you with a sense that all is well. The lightness of spirit that Uranus brings will help you to accept this new awareness without anxiety. Spirituality can overcome both mental and physical constraints.

Uranus brings universal truth. Let this energy put you in touch with the universe. Treasure each day with joy, and take the time to see the beauty in the world around you. Memorize the joy you feel so that you can bring it to mind at will.

Aletha has this to say:

> It's hard for me to get to church now, but my church has a pro-
> gram where visitors come on Sunday to people who have to stay
> at home. Sometimes the minister comes, and sometimes it's one
> of the ladies. They bring me some of the flowers from the altar.
> We say some prayers together, and I really almost like it better
> than going to church—these days I fall asleep during the sermon.
> I have my own prayers and thoughts for every day, of course. It's
> not just Sunday that is holy, but every day.

THE BIRTHDAY

Make an expedition to some interesting place nearby that you've been meaning to visit but haven't got around to before—a rose garden, the zoo, an art gallery. Take your time as you move around and decide on your "favorite thing." Then take a mental photograph—observe it carefully and impress the image on your mind. Take that image home with you as one of the gifts for this day, and when you gaze into the lighted candles on your cake, remember it.

Eighty-six

I F YOU CAN GET THROUGH THIS THIRD SATURN RETURN, you are set to reach your nineties. Depending on how well your personal destiny supports your health, you are now a venerable Elder, balancing naps with getting out into the world. Take care of your memory. The other part of the secret is mental stimulation. Z's Aunt Titi dug a collection of French pharmaceutical magazines out of her closet in order to brush up her command of the language. Many good thinkers are using the winds of change brought by Uranus to take up their work once more.

Your path now is shaped by what you have learned from life. Everything that has happened to you becomes meaningful now. Spend your days in a balanced pattern of walking, bathing, reading, TV, napping, and eating healthy food. Talk to loved ones. Go to bed and enjoy your dreams.

At this age, thinking about those who have already crossed over is natural. You miss your old friends and family. You wonder why you are still around when they have all gone. There is no answer to this question. Count your blessings, enjoy your opportunities, and make friends with those who are still here. But don't avoid thinking about death—that awareness makes life more valuable.

Estelle, who spends some time at the senior center almost every day, says it does get depressing when familiar faces are suddenly gone. What she does is to get some kind of flower and plant it in the center's garden. She says that people aren't really gone so long as their memories bloom.

THE BIRTHDAY

If you miss loved ones whom you've lost, invite them to share your birthday. Take out their pictures and put them on the table. Light a candle for them, and set out a piece of birthday cake. If you think this will make your living friends feel uncomfortable, do this in private. But if you believe they can cope, bring the pictures to the party and tell your friends who everyone was and what they did. What is remembered, lives.

Eighty-seven

Y OU'VE HAD A LONG LIFE. This year, take the opportunity to review your personal history. Remember each decade. What were you doing? Who were your friends? Who did you love? Looking back, you can see how much you have learned and grown. See how rich your heart has been and still is. Congratulations!

Be careful with your health, but not to the point of hypochondria. Life needs death in order to create more life, and no amount of care will change that. Life is both relentless and fair. Live each day as if it were your last, and you will have no regrets.

You should also take care of your property. Make sure your will is up to date. Then search your memory—is there anything that hasn't been settled yet? Do all your heirs know what to expect? Rather than saying, "After I'm gone, you'll get this or that," give away as much as you can while you're still around to watch them enjoy it. It's a bad idea to tempt people with the promise of an inheritance—they can't help hoping, just a little, that you will die soon. You can't take it with you, so be generous, so long as you have kept back enough to live on for the next ten years or so. If you make it to a hundred, you'll be such a celebrity they'll be glad to provide for you!

One little-known secret of old age is its effect on psychic abilities. You may find an increasing tendency to daydream, to detach yourself from present reality. So long as you can snap back and deal with life when needed, don't fight it. Take advantage of your new ability to move between levels of reality. Talk to the spirit world—it's entertainment for the mind. Don't be afraid you're going bonkers—you're expanding your mind. Talk to yourself or to those you see, welcome them into your life. Don't take medications that will dull your imagination—it's one of the most valuable capacities you have left. Age cannot touch it.

Not everyone, however, is focused on the spirit world. At this age, the experience of men and women is much the same. At eighty-seven, William has lost a foot to diabetes, but he has learned to walk on a prosthetic. He lives in the house in the country where he retired with his second wife, who he outlived as he outlived the first, and he still cuts his own wood. He also keeps a sharp eye on his investments. He believes that younger people need to look for conservative investments in companies that will last. At his age, he says, he's learned to take a really long view.

THE BIRTHDAY

By now you should have learned to delegate the effort of putting your birthday party together. Ask for a cake with a bigger candle for each decade and seven small ones. Tell your loved ones what you remember from each decade as you blow them out.

Eighty-eight

B Y THIS YEAR, Saturn has moved out of your natal sign at last. Congratulations on completing the Third Destiny! You are one of a select group who has the option of undertaking a fourth mission in your lives. The planets are giving you a break this year. Take a deep breath and think about what you have learned. Up to this point, you were still an Elder-in-Training. Now you are a graduate. You've been there and done that. You've paid your dues. Now you are free.

Free of what, you may ask, or free to do what?

Well, for one thing, you are free to speak your mind. After all, what can they do to you?

Lorraine didn't feel like responding to our questionnaire, so she didn't. "Figure it out for yourself!" And then she smiled a secret sort of smile that made us wonder, "What does she know?"

Diana's grandmother, when told that the Libby ancestors she had always thought were English were probably Welsh, and that the Welsh were a wonderful people, famous for poetry and music, responded, "Really? I guess I'll tell it that way from now on."

People who were always quite proper may lose their inhibitions. Z's Aunt Titi is fond of a Hungarian saying that translates, "I may be old, but I still have a hole in my ass. . . ." There can be a perverse and particular pleasure in shocking one's descendents.

THE BIRTHDAY

Do something outrageous. Wear purple, or a startling hat. Have plenty to eat and drink. Require each of your guests to describe the funniest thing that ever happened to them. Ask for a children's party with party hats and favors. Invite some children and play games with them.

Eighty-nine

AT EIGHTY-NINE, you are a not only a senior citizen, you are a citizen of your century, and a citizen of the world. Physically you may not be getting around as much any more, but that's no excuse for letting your mind get flabby. In fact, mental calisthenics are even more necessary than physical exercise.

The brain is the only organ that will actually add new cells if it gets the right stimulation. So do puzzles, learn a language, play games like chess that force you to concentrate. Make sure you get plenty of brain food to support all this activity—ginkgo biloba, complex carbohydrates, B-vitamins, and vitamin E. Your short-term memory may not be what it was, but your powers of concentration and your judgment improve with the years.

Lorraine says, "What I like most about this age is being able to please myself. I go to the senior center three times a week. I enjoy the yoga class and I'm also taking a class in Sign Language so that I can interpret for the deaf. The movement is good exercise for my hands. But sometimes I take a vacation from the classes and just stay home and do things around the house."

THE BIRTHDAY

Expose yourself to new ideas. Read an unusual book or see an avant-garde film even, or especially, if you think you won't like it. Take a few risks. What do you have to lose? By the end of this day you should be able to say that you know at least one thing you didn't know before.

Ninety

SO, HERE YOU ARE WITH NINE times ten candles on your cake. You've had ninety chances to see the sun come round to your natal day, ninety years filled with living and learning.

Mollie writes that being ninety

> *feels wonderful. I've had so many experiences and enjoy meeting younger people. I've learned to compromise, be more flexible, understanding the new way people share their lives. There are so many new technologies, the computer, cell phone, the ways that people can get in touch with each other. They even have e-mail so that in a matter of minutes you can contact someone. Families are different, even with one parent people manage to live together and love each other. As I said before, I wouldn't go back for even one day. I look forward to my life being enriched. I still take piano lessons.*

THE BIRTHDAY

At the age of ninety, Diana's grandmother celebrated with a ride in a motorcycle sidecar, followed by a formal dinner attended by most of her descendents. She had a wonderful dress of plum-colored lace, and she looked absolutely beautiful.

This is certainly a birthday that deserves a splendid celebration—a new dress, your favorite foods, as many friends and family members as you can fit in. On this day you are not merely a queen, you are Empress. Wear a tiara. Enter the dining room on the arm of a good-looking man or attended by ladies.

This is a good time to share the high points of your life with those you love. Before the party, go through old photos and put together an album. Instead of trying to fit ninety candles on your cake, ask for nine brightly colored candles, plus one for the time to come. When it's time to blow them out, talk about each decade. Where did you live, and with whom? Who did you love? What made you happy or unhappy? Tell a favorite story about something that happened during that time, and then blow the candle out. When you are finished, set the extra candle aside and let it burn throughout the rest of the party.

The Fourth Destiny

WHAT DO WE KNOW ABOUT THE FOURTH DESTINY? Mostly, what we have is questions. If someone asks whether old age is a joy or a burden, the answer will probably be "Yes." According to psychoanalyst Erik Erikson, the eighth stage of adult development is a conflict between integrity and despair. Poor health, the loss or illness of loved ones, and economic fears may cause chronic anxiety. By this time, most of your decisions are behind you. You can't change them. All you can do is learn to accept and take responsibility for what you have done with your life. It's necessary to forgive yourself and release any guilt you are still carrying. There is no point in measuring yourself against others. You are who you are. It is time to learn to accept and enjoy it.

There are a lot of wise words that sound like platitudes until you reach an age where they are literally true. If life is not always pleasant, at least time is passing quickly. By the time you reach your mid-eighties, disasters may have less power to upset you because you've seen it all before and know that life goes on. You can afford to tolerate ambiguity now, and to live and let live.

Shez writes:

> One of my uncles, who is over ninety, still works. He teaches art on cruise liners and teaches night classes on art. He has quite an eye for the ladies and they have quite an eye for him. My mother and father were ballroom dancing in their seventies. My mum still goes dancing and loves parties. I come from a family of people who never stopped living until the day they died, and I feel I will probably be the same way.

Anna, whom we interviewed at the senior center yoga class, responded that the secret to an active, happy life at ninety-six is to live for the day. She's surprised to have gotten this far. She's been married for seventy-one years, and she and her husband are still living in their home. She says that it's hard to tell others how to live.

Being active and interacting both physically and mentally with other people is important. Artist Georgia O'Keefe continued producing memorable work until her ninety-eighth year. Labor organizer "Mother" Jones, who made it to one hundred, was a hell-raiser to the end.

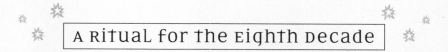

A Ritual for the Eighth Decade

WALKING INTO THE SUNRISE: A PROCESS FOR RE-CREATING THE SELF

It took nine months to create the physical body in which your soul has been living all these years. It takes almost nine decades to mature your soul. Like your body, your soul has grown and changed during that time. In traditional Hindu culture, the first part of life is spent as a student, the second as a parent and householder, and the third, withdrawing from the world to perfect the spirit. With old age comes enlightenment.

At this point you may start to laugh, "Enlightened? Well, it's true I know a few things, but mostly what I've learned is how much I don't know. . . ."

According to many spiritual teachers, that *is* the essence of enlighten-ment. The secret lies not so much in admitting ignorance, but in a willingness to be still, and accept that you are a part of the unfolding life of the universe, whose true nature will always be a mystery. It is no longer necessary to con-trol life, but only to enjoy it.

In your mid-eighties, Saturn has cycled around three times, a magic number. Three is the number that brings time and space together. With your third Saturn Return you complete the achievements of your life and can look beyond.

For the first and second Saturn Returns, we suggested inviting friends and family to support and witness your passage. But the significance of this third Saturn ritual is self-realization. You still love others. You depend on them for many things, as they depend on you. But your spirit has become complete in itself.

Thus, this working is for you alone. Not only can others be a distraction, it may be hard for them to comprehend the inner changes you have been experiencing. You don't have the spare energy to spend on making them understand, and, frankly, they don't really need to know. The spiritual litera-ture of many lands describes the meditations of the wise as solitary. You are blazing a new trail into the secret country. How much you choose to let others know about your discoveries, and when you share it, is up to you. Because you will be working alone, the pace and timing are your choice as well.

PART I

Begin where you are, with a review of your Third Destiny. Before beginning the soul work, evaluate your life from a medical, legal and economic, and physical perspective.

If you are not seeing a doctor regularly, schedule an appointment. Check everything, not only the aspects of your health that you know are problem-atic, but the systems that are working well. Give your body the equivalent of a complete systems check on a car. What is in good shape? What is not in good shape but can be fixed? What problems are you just going to have to live with?

Subject your economic health to the same kind of analysis. Look at your assets and your liabilities. If you have a financial advisor, go over your investments. Sit down with your lawyer and make any revisions necessary in your will. What resources do you have, and how can you make them serve you for another dozen years?

Take this opportunity to conduct an equally comprehensive survey of your home. What needs to be fixed or replaced, and what will last? What things do you really need to keep, either for your own use or for posterity, and what can you get rid of now? For this task, you can use help from a younger friend or relative who can still lift all those boxes. The benefits of a thorough cleaning will probably be quite apparent without any need to explain why you are doing it.

Don't make a clean sweep. You are happier with your own things around you, but there are some things—unimportant correspondence, outdated financial records, old clothing, many of those bits and pieces that "just might come in handy someday"—that really should go. After all, one of these days someone will have to make the decision on what is valuable and what to do with it. Wouldn't you rather it was you? At the same time, you can make a list of who should eventually receive the keepsakes you are saving—things whose value is more sentimental than monetary and that will not be listed in your will.

By the time you have finished with all this, you may feel exhausted, but you will probably feel a great sense of relief as well. You have cleared the decks and set down a burden.

Make a space on top of a cabinet or table and cover it with a handsome cloth. Even a linen handkerchief, a silk scarf, or a new tea towel will do. On the cloth, set a candle and a picture of yourself taken in the past fifteen years. Light the candle so that it illuminates the picture. Sit comfortably and contemplate it. Take a piece of paper or turn on a tape recorder and describe the woman you are now. What are her assets, in health, friends, economic resources, and so on, and what are her liabilities? Think about what you have said for a little while, and then find three words to represent yourself. Write them on a card and place them on your altar.

PART II

You'll probably want to take a breather after the first part of this working. The next part, in which you deal with your Second Destiny, will be less demanding physically, but it may be harder on the emotions. In this section, you are going to "mother" yourself.

The years of your Second Destiny were probably the time when you were most active and most in charge of your life. In fact you may have been so active, and spent so much time taking care of others, that you had little time for soulwork. Find photos of yourself during that period and gather them together with other memorabilia. Who was that woman? What were her hopes and fears?

You have now reached or passed the age that your own mother was when you were in your Second Destiny. Unless you were very fortunate, you never had the kind of conversation with your mother that you would like to have had. If you have children of your own, you may well find it difficult to share your inner life with them, and vice versa. But the woman you are now can mother the woman you were then.

How can you reach her? You may have changed, but she still lives within. Sit down and write her a letter. Contemplate the woman in the photos, and send a message that will transcend time and touch her soul. What mistakes did she make? What were her triumphs? And which of both have turned out, as time passes, to have been less important than they seemed? Write her words of comfort. If there are old errors that can be set right, promise restitution. But what is more likely is that many of those traumas will in retrospect have dwindled to the size of a hurt finger or a skinned knee. Hold that hurt woman in your heart and give her a mother's comfort and forgiveness.

Comfort is not all you have to offer. Give also the praise you would have liked to hear from your own mother. What actions of your Second Destiny had good results, perhaps eventual outcomes that were much more important than they seemed at the time? Assure your younger self that she did well, that her efforts were not in vain.

When you have finished, put the letter on your altar, and in a vase, next to the candle, put one of your favorite flowers.

PART III

The Navajo have legends of a divine figure called Changing Woman, who brought many great gifts to the People. When she grows old, she walks toward the sunrise until she becomes young once more. When you have rested a little, it will be time to think about the third part of this soulwork, rebirthing the child within. Your joints are probably not up to any recapitulation of physical childhood, but the purpose is to re-create your spirit, not your body.

Spend some time thinking about childhood. If necessary, reread the first and second chapter of this book to refresh your memory. In addition to eating, sleeping, and getting a great deal of exercise, what do children do? They learn, they play, and they pay attention to the world.

It's time for you to do the same once more.

Learning is easiest. You can choose any area of knowledge that interests you, or you can simply take a dictionary, let it fall open at random, and go down the page until you find an unusual word you do not know. If the game amuses you, do this several times until you have a number of new words to play with. Roll them on your tongue. Make up sentences in which to use them. Over the next several days, look for opportunities to use them in conversation.

Next comes play. From a catalog or a toy store choose a children's game (you can always say you are purchasing it for your grandchildren). Then, play it. If it requires more than one participant, play against yourself, or persuade someone else to join you. The simpler, and to some extent sillier, the game the better. The point is to relax and release your inhibitions and live in the moment.

This should help you with the third task, which is to re-experience the wonder of the world. For one day, decide that you will look upon everything, hear, touch, and taste everything, as if you have never encountered it before. The very young and the very old can get away with actions, such as talking to oneself, that are forbidden to those in the middle of life. If it helps you to fully integrate the experience, verbalize it. Exclaim with wonder. Don't be afraid to be thought childish—it will be true, though not in the way people think. Place some symbol of what you have experienced—an interesting rock, a leaf, a toy—on the altar you have made.

Afterward, you can resume your dignity, but remember that freshness of perception and sense of freedom. Once it has served its purpose, you can dismantle your altar. When the reality is a part of you, the symbols will not matter anymore. The radiance of eternity shines through children, who are still close to their beginning. As your life comes full circle, you are nearing your beginning as well, and can allow your eternal spirit to show through.

AFTERWORD

Looking for the Meaning of Life

WHAT IS THE MEANING OF LIFE? That's a question that in every age, both historical and personal, we find ourselves compelled to ask. Life is a challenging job, and we have to write our own instruction manuals for getting through it. We teach each other some things. We know, for example, that although everybody's life has a different plot, they all have the same ending. Our bodies are going to break down. A walk through the cemetery makes that quite clear. Here they all are—the rich and the poor, the successful and the unknown, man and woman and child, all equal at the end.

So why do we struggle? Can't we just "let it be"; "Don't worry, be happy!"? Why do we half-kill ourselves with jobs and service to others? Why not just find a low-stress road and stay on it until we draw our final breaths?

We may dream of taking it easy, but deep down, we know that this journey through life has a meaning beyond just getting by, and it's our job to find it. Searching for the meaning of life means embarking on a spiritual path. This spiritual striving is instinctive, deeply seated in our hearts, not necessarily logical, but always compelling. We need creativity, even when it brings pain. We need a vigorous inner life. And we need a higher kind of love—this is the ultimate romance. Our spiritual path can provide us with a road map that shows us how to live, how to be happy, how to love, how to die. We want to do this journey right. We crave for a glimpse of the Plan.

After all, if every molecule, every atom, every proton and electron seem to know what they're doing and where to go, surely we should be the same. The great systems of which everything is a part interlock and interact in perfect harmony. So what if we can't see the plan—80 percent of the universe is invisible because it doesn't reflect light we can see with our eyes. If we are to truly understand the universe, we have to learn to see with our spirits.

In fact, we ourselves are a universe in which millions of cells live and die. Clusters of cells have died while you were reading this page, and many more were born. Whether or not they know what they are doing, they cooperate in keeping our bodies going. When they die, their elements pass into the outer universe to become a part of other things. When Hamlet contemplates the process by which the dust of a beggar can become part of a Caesar, he is confirming this inter-connectedness of all things. In the play, this knowledge doesn't seem to give him much consolation, but Hamlet still has a young man's illu-sions. One of the gifts of age is the ability to see both ourselves and our world in perspective.

Humans are unique not because we are outside or above the system, but because we are self-aware. We not only obey the universal law of growth and change, but we have the potential to consciously partici-pate in the process. We feel the need to understand this, we want to cooperate as the universal will unfolds. This spiritual purpose is already manifesting within us. The purpose of life is for us to notice that it's there, understand it better, and celebrate it a lot!

The best way to look for the meaning of life is in company with other seekers. We see each other more clearly than we see ourselves. In each other's eyes, we find mirrors in which to behold ourselves. It is not only lovers who do this, but companions as well. We are remarkably alike in pain and in joy. We share the same experiences in birth and in death. The rest is window dressing.

Our lives are a dance in which we create our own figures within a larger pattern. The larger planets create the dance, but the best dancers are those who understand the structure of the dance, and the meaning of the music—the more we know about our heredity, environment, and the spiritual forces that govern our lives, the better we will be able to understand our options and choose wisely among them. The pattern of the dance may be preordained, but we choose how to perform.

That, one might say, is the Meaning, the Mystery of Life. We can't know everything about the accidents, the serendipitous blessings or curses that mold our lives, but the more we understand, the better able we will be to learn from what happens to us and ride the wave of the future instead of being swept away.

We learn from mythology and science, from astrology and ritual. Above all, we have learned from the words of those who are walking with us on this path. The women and men who shared their experiences with us help us understand where we are going and where we have been. They are the ones who are paying attention to what's happening and trying to understand its meaning. Together, we are creating a map of life for others to follow.

This map is drawn with bold strokes, leaving plenty of blank space for each one of us to fill in with her own choices. Some parts say, "Here there be monsters," but even the monsters, if you confront them boldly, may give you a blessing. Pain can be a teacher—without it a child cannot be born or grow up.

What it won't do is lead us into the so-called White Light. White Light brings to mind an over-lit New Age universe. If the light is too bright, or the darkness too black, we can't see anything. We're better off with natural light and shadow. Shadow makes light visible, and light shows where the shadows are.

Look through the lens of destiny. Peer deeply into the infinite. You will see a nebula, new suns, billions of stars in the Milky Way. We stand on the green Earth, amid blue skies and hummingbirds, flowering gardens and all the other beings with which we share the planet. The better we understand how we fit into the circle of life, the more grateful we will feel at the opportunity to be co-creators of destiny.

At this "meta-level," there are some limitations on free will. If you are living in the sub-age of Aquarius, you cannot change it into the sub-age of Aries, no matter how hard you try. Each age has a "zeitgeist," a spirit of the times. It is this current of time in which we must learn to swim, like fish in a river.

Where free will comes in is not whether we are going to swim, but how, or to shift metaphors, if Time is the architect that has created the splendid Age in which we are living, then we are the interior decorators. We put in the windows and the curtains and the furniture. But whatever we do, the building will stand; the river will flow.

Death is the ultimate democracy, treating the rich and the poor equally. From the stars, there are only various species, living together on a blue planet. From the perspective of the stars, what matters is that the species continues. If humans survive, we can evolve as a collective consciousness. Ours is the species with the responsibility for caring for all the others. Civilizations can flower. Only consciousness can create a paradise on Earth. Everyone has to participate to complete the job. No one will be left behind.

It is time to abandon war as a means of settling differences. As the Dalai Lama has pointed out, war is obsolete, and it's human consciousness that needs changing. Real victories are won only when consciousness is raised.

This is an evolution that cannot be halted, no matter how some may try. Propaganda, brainwashing, religion, media dis-information—all, in the end, will fail to suppress the truth. Our collective consciousness demands knowledge. Our minds are inherently curious. When we learn, we, as people of the planet, change our world and ourselves. Curiously, these changes often coincide with the visits of the transpersonal planets.

How do these universal forces work? Well, let's call it the Cosmic Dust Bunny Theory. You clean your hardwood floors—mop and wipe them until they shine. A few days later, you begin to see particles gathering. Where are they coming from? You don't allow dirt on your clean floors. But the particles float unseen through the air, drawn by some unseen force to gather together. They drift like thoughts, and if you don't disperse them quickly with a mop, they gather into increasingly organized societies, swirling together in a spiral pattern until in a few days you can hold them in your hand. Contemplate them with awe. Just as the invisible cosmic dust of the universe coalesced to form planets, or stray thoughts organize themselves into ideas and then action, the dust bunnies have captured infinity.

We move through our lives to the music of the spheres. It's a long, long dance, each year a different step, but we have time to learn....

GLOSSARY

conjunction Two planets are located within 8° of each other. When a planet conjuncts itself, it is returning to its natal position. In this position, its influence is intensified.

destiny The experiences and actions to which your environment, character, age, and astrological configurations predispose you, shaped by the choices you make. During each Saturn cycle you may have a different destiny.

fate Often used as a synonym for *destiny;* the Roman name for one of the goddesses who ordains it.

hinge The years during which Saturn is passing through the position on your astrological chart he occupied at the time you were born.

mission The work that your own character and the needs of the time in which you live push you to do during a given Saturn cycle.

moon sign The sign of the zodiac in which the moon appeared at the time you were born. It governs *emotions and instincts,* and affects *family and love relationships.*

movement The shift of a planet from one sign of the zodiac to another.

natal position The place on your astrological chart occupied by a planet at the time you were born.

nodes of the moon The two points marking the farthest extremes of the moon's orbit through the ecliptic (the orbit of the Earth around the sun). Some astrologers state that *the northern node brings positive energy and points you toward your job in this life,* *while the southern is more restrictive.* Others say that *the south node indicates patterns and talents from past lives that we revert to under stress.*

nodes of Saturn The points marking the extremes of Saturn's orbit.

Norns Urdh (or Wyrd), Verdandi, and Skuld, the northern European equivalent of the Three Fates.

opposition (astrological) A planet is at 180°, or directly across the circle of the chart, from another. In this book, usually this means in opposition to its natal position. This position can cause blockage or misunderstanding. It is necessary to strive for a deeper awareness to find a point of harmony. Opposition may also include an opportunity to reach agreement regarding the misunderstandings, even if you only agree to disagree.

quincunx An "inconjunction" or angle of 150° between one planet and another (or between it and its natal position), causing the energy to waver and become confused. Conflicts are unconscious, making it hard to address them.

return A planet completes one cycle through the zodiac and returns to its natal position in your chart.

rising sign (also called the ascendant) The zodiacal constellation (sign) that was rising above the horizon when you were born. It shapes your body and affects the way you react to the world—it is part of your "act."

Saturn cycle The 28-to-30-year period required for Saturn to cycle through the entire zodiac and return to his natal position on your chart. Many people find their lives changing significantly after each cycle.

sextile (astrological) A planet is at an angle of 60° to another (or to its natal position), a position of cooperative and productive energy.

square (astrological) A planet is at an angle of 90° to another (or to its natal position), causing conflict of interest expressed internally. Working to rise above the conflict can bring positive change, because the square is a catalyst for changes that you yourself cause.

sun sign The sign of the zodiac in which the sun appeared when you were born. This is where your energy comes from. It affects your will and intellect and the way you relate to the exterior world. It is part of your "real" self.

transit Movement of a planet from one sign to another.

trine (astrological) A planet is at an angle of 120° to another (or to its natal position), allowing for a harmonious relationship and flow of energy.

RESOURCES
General Books and Periodicals

Sheila Belanger, "Homeward Bound: An Astrological Perspective on Women's Mid-life Cycles," *The Beltane Papers Magazine* 10. Lammas, P.O. Box 29694, Bellingham, WA 98228-1694.

Blessed Bee: A Pagan Family Newsletter. Box 641, Point Arena, CA 95468.

Z Budapest, *Grandmother of Time.* San Francisco: Harper, 1989.

_____, *Grandmother Moon.* San Francisco: Harper, 1991.

_____, *The Holy Book of Women's Mysteries.* Berkeley: Wingbow Press, 1980, 1989.

_____, *Summoning the Fates.* New York: Harmony Books, 1998.

Jane Caputi, *Gossips, Gorgons, Crones: The Fates of the Earth.* Santa Fe, NM: Bear & Co., 1993.

Phyllis Chesler, *Woman's Inhumanity to Woman.* New York: Thundermouth Press/Nation Books, 2002.

Simone De Beauvoir, *The Second Sex,* trans. H. M. Parshley. New York: Vintage Books, 1989.

Susan Faludi, *Backlash: The Undeclared War Against American Women.* New York: Doubleday Anchor, 1992.

Deborah G. Felder, *The 100 Most Influential Women of All Time.* New York: Citadel Press, 1996.

Betty Friedan, *The Feminine Mystique.* New York: W. W. Norton, 1963, 2001.

_____, *The Fountain of Age.* New York: Simon & Schuster, 1993.

_____, *The Second Stage.* New York: Summit Books, 1981.

Arnold Gesell and Frances L. Ilg, *The Child From Five to Ten.* New York: Harper & Brothers, 1946.

Arnold Gesell, Frances L. Ilg, Louise B. Ames, *Youth: The Years from Ten to Sixteen.* New York: Harper & Brothers, 1956.

Geraldine Hatch Hanon, *Sacred Space, A Feminist Vision of Astrology.* Ithaca, NY: Firebrand Books, 1990.

Modern Maturity. 601 E Street, Washington, DC 20049.

Thomas Moore, *Care of the Soul.* New York: Harper-Collins, 1992.

Diana L. Paxson (with Marion Zimmer Bradley), *Priestess of Avalon.* New York: Viking Press, 2001.

Sagewoman. Box 641, Point Arena, CA 95468.

Gail Sheehy, *New Passages.* New York: Random House, 1995.

Rachel Simmons, *Odd Girl Out: The Hidden Culture of Aggression in Girls.* New York: Harcourt Brace, 2002.

Michael Thompson, Catherine O'Neill Grace, Lawrence J. Cohen, *Best Friends, Worst Enemies: Understanding the Emotional Lives of Children.* New York: Ballantine Books, 2001.

Alison Weir and Susan Raven, *Women of Achievement: Thirty-five Centuries of History.* Boston: Beacon Press, 1984.

Susun S. Weed, *Menopausal Years.* Woodstock, NY: Ash Tree Publishing, 1992.

Melissa Gayle West, *Exploring the Labyrinth.* New York: Broadway Books, 2000.

Emily White, *Fast Girls: Teenage Tribes and the Myth of the Slut.* New York: Scribners, 2002.

Rosalind Wiseman, *Queen Bees and Wannabees: Helping Your Daughter Survive Cliques, Gossip, Boyfriends and Other Realities of Adolescence.* New York: Crown Books, 2002.

Books on Astrology

Linda Brady and Evan St. Lifer, *Discovering Your Soul Mission*. New York: Three Rivers Press, 1998.

Liz Greene, *The Astrology of Fate*. York Beach, ME: Samuel Weiser, 1984.

William W. Hewitt, *Astrology for Beginners*. Minneapolis: Llewellyn, 2002.

Alan Oken, *Alan Oken's Complete Astrology* (includes *As Above, So Below; The Horoscope;* and *Astrology: Evolution and Revolution*). New York: Bantam, 1988.

Julia Parker, *The Astrologer's Handbook*. Sebastopol, CA: CRCS Publishing, 1995.

Erin Sullivan, *Planets in Transit*. London: Arkana, 1991.

Joanna Martine Woolfolk, *The Only Astrology Book You'll Ever Need*. New York: Madison Books, 2001.

Web Sites

The American Association of Retired People
www.aarp.org/index.html

Astrology Sites
www.alabe.com
www.astrology.net

Goddess Statues
www.MythicImages.com

The Gray Panthers
www.graypanthers.org

Music

Gustav Holst, *The Planets* (many good recordings are available).